919

JL

The Invasion of Normandy

Books in the Battle Series:

★ ★ ★ Battles of World War II ★ ★ ★

The Invasion of Normandy

by David Pietrusza

Lucent Books, P.O. Box 289011, San Diego, CA 92198-9011

Library of Congress Cataloging-in-Publication Data

Pietrusza, David, 1949–
    The Invasion of Normandy / by David Pietrusza.
        p.   cm. — (Battles of World War II)
    Includes bibliography and index.
    ISBN 1-56006-413-7   (lib. ed. : alk. paper)
    1. World War, 1939–1945—Campaigns—France—Normandy—Juvenile
literature.   2. Normandy (France)—History, Military—Juvenile literature.
[1. World War, 1939–1945—Campaigns—France—Normandy.
2. Normandy (France)—History, Military.]   I. Title.   II. Series.
D756.5.N6P475   1996
940.54'21—dc20
                                                95-12205
                                                  CIP
                                                     AC

Contents

Foreword

Almost everyone would agree with William Tecumseh Sherman that war "is all hell." Yet the history of war, and battles in particular, is so fraught with the full spectrum of human emotion and action that it becomes a microcosm of the human experience. Soldiers' lives are condensed and crystallized in a single battle. As Francis Miller explains in his *Photographic History of the Civil War* when describing the war wounded, "It is sudden, the transition from marching bravely at morning on two sound legs, grasping your rifle in two sturdy arms, to lying at nightfall under a tree with a member forever gone."

Decisions made on the battlefield can mean the lives of thousands. A general's pique or indigestion can result in the difference between life and death. Some historians speculate, for example, that Napoleon's fateful defeat at Waterloo was due to the beginnings of stomach cancer. His stomach pain may have been the reason that the normally decisive general was sluggish and reluctant to move his troops. And what kept George McClellan from winning battles during the Civil War? Some scholars and contemporaries believe that it was simple cowardice and fear. Others argue that he felt a gut-wrenching unwillingness to engage in the war of attrition that was characteristic of that particular conflict.

Battle decisions can be magnificently brilliant and horribly costly. At the Battle of Thaspus in 47 B.C., for example, Julius Caesar, facing a numerically superior army, shrewdly ordered his troops onto a narrow strip of land bordering the sea. Just as he expected, his enemy thought he had accidentally trapped himself and divided their forces to surround his troops. By dividing their army, his enemy had given Caesar the strategic edge he needed to defeat them. Other battle orders result in disaster, as in the case of the Battle at Balaklava during the Crimean War in 1854. A British general gave the order to attack a force of withdrawing enemy Russians. But confusion in relaying the order resulted in the 670 men of the Light Brigade's charging in the wrong direction into certain death by heavy enemy cannon fire. Battles are the stuff of history on the grandest scale—their outcomes often determine whether nations are enslaved or liberated.

Moments in battles illustrate the best and worst of human character. In the feeling of terror and the us-versus-them attitude that accompanies war, the enemy can be dehumanized and treated with a contempt that is considered repellent in times of peace. At Wounded Knee, the distrust and anticipation of violence that grew between the Native Americans and American soldiers led to the senseless killing of ninety men, women, and children. And who can forget My Lai, where the deaths of old men, women, and children at the hands of American soldiers shocked an America already disillusioned with the Vietnam War. The murder of six million Jews will remain burned into the human conscience forever as the measure of man's inhumanity to man. These horrors cannot be forgotten. And yet, under the terrible conditions of battle, one can find acts of bravery, kindness, and altruism. During the Battle of Midway, the members of Torpedo Squadron 8, flying in hopelessly antiquated planes and without the benefit of air protection from fighters, tried bravely to fulfill their mission—to destroy the *Kido Butai,* the Japanese Carrier Striking Force. Without air support, the squadron was immediately set upon by Japanese fighters. Nevertheless, each bomber tried valiantly to hit his target. Each failed. Every man but one died in the effort. But by keeping the Japanese fighters busy, the squadron bought time and delayed further Japanese fighter attacks. In the aftermath of the Battle of Isandhlwana in South Africa in 1879, a force of thousands of Zulu warriors trapped a contingent of British troops in a small trading post. After repeated bloody attacks in which many died on both sides, the Zulus, their final victory certain, granted the remaining British their lives as a gesture of respect for their bravery. During World War I, American troops were so touched by the fate of French war orphans that they took up a collection to help them. During the Civil War, soldiers of the North and South would briefly forget that they were enemies and share smokes and coffee across battle lines during the endless nights. These acts seem all the more dramatic, more uplifting, because they indicate that people can continue to behave with humanity when faced with inhumanity.

Lucent Books' Battles Series highlights the vast range of the human character revealed in the ordeal of war. Dramatic narrative describes in exciting and accurate detail the commanders, soldiers, weapons, strategies, and maneuvers involved in each battle. Each volume includes a comprehensive historical context, explaining what brought the parties to war, the events leading to the battle, what factors made the battle important, and the effects it had on the larger war and later events.

The Battles Series also includes a chronology of important dates that gives students an overview, at a glance, of each battle. Sidebars create a broader context by adding enlightening details on leaders, institutions, customs, warships, weapons, and armor mentioned in the narration. Every volume contains numerous maps that allow readers to better visualize troop movements and strategies. In addition, numerous primary and secondary source quotations drawn from both past historical witnesses and modern historians are included. These quotations demonstrate to readers how and where historians derive information about past events. Finally, the volumes in the Battles Series provide a launching point for further reading and research. Each book contains a bibliography designed for student research, as well as a second bibliography that includes the works the author consulted while compiling the book.

Above all, the Battles Series helps illustrate the words of Herodotus, the fifth-century B.C. Greek historian now known as the "father of history." In the opening lines of his great chronicle of the Greek and Persian Wars, the world's first battle book, he set for himself this goal: "To preserve the memory of the past by putting on record the astonishing achievements both of our own and of other peoples; and more particularly, to show how they came into conflict."

Chronology of Events

1918

September   Hitler joins German Workers Party (later National Socialist German Workers Party).

November 11   Germany surrenders. World War I ends.

1923

November 8–9   "Beer Hall Putsch" fails in Munich.

1933

January 30   Hitler takes power in Germany.

1934

August 19   Hitler becomes "Führer and Reich Chancellor."

1936

March 7   German troops reenter the Rhineland.

1938

March 11–13   Germany absorbs Austria.

September 29–30   Munich Conference decides fate of Czechoslovakia.

1939

March 15   German troops enter rest of Czechoslovakia.

August 23   Germany and the Soviet Union sign Non-Aggression Pact.

September 1   Germany invades Poland.

September 3   United Kingdom and France declare war on Germany.

September 17   Soviet Union invades Poland.

November 28   Soviet Union invades Finland.

1940

April 9   Germany invades Denmark and Norway.

May 10   German blitzkrieg begins in the West; Churchill becomes British prime minister.

May 26–June 14   British evacuate army from Dunkirk.

June 14   Paris falls to the Germans.

June 22   France signs armistice with Germany.

August 1940–May 1941   Battle of Britain.

1941

February   Rommel placed in command of Afrika Korps.

June 22   Germany invades the Soviet Union.

December 7   Japan attacks Pearl Harbor.

December 11   Germany declares war on United States.

1942

August 17   Canadians raid Dieppe.

October 23–November 5   Montgomery stops Rommel at El Alamein.

November 11   Germany occupies Vichy France.

1943

January 31   Von Paulus surrenders at Stalingrad.

May   Plan for invasion of Europe given code name Operation Overlord.

July 10   Allies invade Sicily.

July 25   Mussolini ousted from power.

December   Eisenhower named to head Operation Overlord; Rommel takes command of German defenses in northwest France.

1944

January 15   Hitler appoints Rommel head of Army Group B.

January 23   Eisenhower approves Montgomery's plans for Normandy landing.

April 28   Slapton Sands training exercise costs 749 American lives.

May 17   Eisenhower sets invasion for early June.

June 2   First Allied ships set out for Normandy.

June 3   All Allied troops aboard ships for invasion; weather around Normandy casts doubt on feasibility of an invasion.

June 4   Weather clears around Normandy.

June 5   Eisenhower's original date for invasion to commence; Eisenhower makes decision to invade on June 6 instead.

2215 Germans intercept message indicating invasion will commence within forty-eight hours.

June 6 D day

0020 Paratroopers begin landings in Normandy.

0035 British glider troops seize Caen Canal bridge at Benouville.

0315 Royal Air Force bombs beach area.

0345 Troops bound for Omaha Beach leave the USS *Henrico* and the HMS *Empire Anvil*.

0400 Hitler retires for the night.

0430 Americans capture the Iles-St.-Marcouf.

0500 Pemsel warns Rommel's headquarters of a "large scale attack"; von Puttkamer decides not to wake Hitler.

0600 Allied naval bombardment of beaches begins.

0630 Americans land at Omaha and Utah Beaches; Rommel receives word only of paratroop landings; Feuchtinger orders his 12th Panzer Division to attack British 6th Airborne.

0725 British land at Gold and Sword Beaches.

0745 Canadians land on Juno Beach.

0800 7th Canadian Brigade lands at Corsuelles.

1000 Rommel receives word of Allied amphibious landings; Hitler awakes at Berchtesgaden; 12th Panzer Division ordered to halt attack on 6th Airborne.

1100 Americans capture Vierville; Taylor rallies the 1st Division at Omaha.

1330 Bradley receives word Americans are moving off the beach at Omaha.

1600 12th Panzer and Panzer Lehr Divisions receive orders to move on Normandy.

2230 Rommel returns to his French headquarters.

June 8 British capture Bayeux; Bayerlein wounded.

June 13 Hitler begins V-1 attacks on Britain.

June 17 Hitler meets with Rommel and von Rundstedt at Soissons.

June 18–21 Mulberry A destroyed by English Channel storm.

June 27 Americans capture Cherbourg.

July 1 Americans capture entire Cherbourg peninsula.

July 10 British and Canadians capture Caen.

July 17 Rommel injured when his car is strafed by Allied planes.

July 18 Allies capture St.-Lo.

July 20 Hitler escapes assassination.

July 25 Bradley begins breakout from Normandy at St.-Lo.

July 31 Allies capture Avranches.

August 4 Patton captures Rennes.

August 15 Allies invade southern France.

August 21 Falaise Gap closed.

August 25 Paris liberated.

October 14 Rommel commits suicide.

December 16 Battle of the Bulge begins.

1945

March 7 Allies capture bridge across Rhine at Remagen.

April 30 Hitler commits suicide.

May 7 Germany surrenders.

The Beginning of the End

It is easy to gloss over the numbers of casualties in World War II. They are so large. Individual suffering and sorrow is overwhelmed by the enormity of statistics. Twenty million soldiers dead. Millions more civilians dead. Hundred of thousands of soldiers captured in single battles such as Stalingrad or Bastogne. Untold millions wounded or displaced on both sides of the conflict.

The Battle of Normandy left thousands dead or wounded on a single day on a stretch of five beaches in the northwestern French province of Normandy. That day was June 6, 1944, D day, the beginning of the British and American invasion of western Europe, the largest amphibious landing in history—and the beginning of the end for Nazi Germany. One hundred and sev-

American soldiers debark from landing barges and storm the beach while moving into fire from Nazi defenders during the D day invasion of the French coast.

enty thousand Allied troops crossed the English Channel to France that day on a fleet that stretched twenty miles across. Of the 5,000 ships included in the invasion force, 1,500 were landing craft and 702 were warships designed to pound the Germans on the French shore into submission.

A Captive Europe

Germany under dictator Adolf Hitler had conquered most of Europe by 1942. Starting with Poland in September 1939 he had moved north to Denmark and Norway and west to the Netherlands, Belgium, Luxembourg, and France. Although his bombing campaign failed to force Britain's surrender, he successfully overran the Balkan nations of Romania, Bulgaria, Yugoslavia, and Greece, and then attacked his former ally, the Soviet Union.

Driven by a notion of Germanic racial superiority, Hitler's rule was merciless. As he saw it, Germans constituted a master race destined to rule other nations. Hitler's Nazis (National Socialists) claimed they needed *lebensraum* ("living space") in the east and set out to destroy the "subhuman" Poles, Ukrainians, and Russians already living there. People of Jewish descent suffered Hitler's strongest hatred. Eventually he conceived and implemented a "final solution," brutally exterminating between five and six million European Jews.

Adolf Hitler (above) had taken over most of Europe before the United States decided to enter the war. (Below) Rescued by conquering troops, these starving Jews fell victim to Hitler's effort to eliminate Jews during the Holocaust.

Operation Overlord

Despite reverses in Russia, North Africa, and Italy, as late as June 1944 Hitler still controlled most of the European continent. Millions of people still suffered Hitler's brutal tyranny. Some were marked for death in the gas chambers; others were starved or worked to death. Most lived in constant fear of their arrogant Nazi conquerors.

To win the war and to liberate the suffering peoples of Europe, Allied British, American, and Canadian armies planned a massive amphibious landing on France's Normandy peninsula for early June 1944. The logistics were complicated. They would have to cross the often-violent English Channel, carefully anticipating such natural phenomena as tides, winds, and moonlight. Once landed the Allies would face a determined German defense bent on destroying fragile beachheads before they were secured.

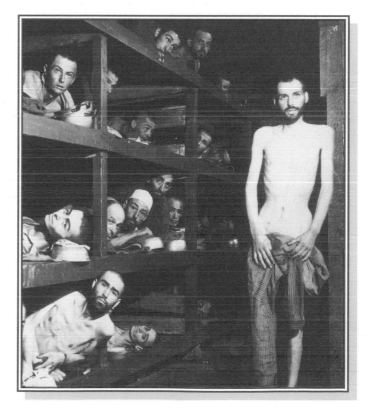

To solve their landing problems, new types of tanks and numerous other vehicles had to be designed and built. The Allies would even tow two huge artificial harbors from England to Normandy to use until they could capture an existing seaport.

The Allies code-named the operation Overlord. They spent six months training hundreds of thousands of soldiers and amassing millions of tons of supplies for the invasion. England became a huge armed camp preparing for D day (the actual day of the first landing). Allied planes relentlessly strafed and bombed German-occupied France to weaken resistance to the invasion.

Exhaustive preparations notwithstanding, success was hardly guaranteed. In August 1942 the Allies had landed unsuccessfully at Dieppe, a port city in northern France, and suffered tremendous losses. Memories of Dieppe continued to haunt them as planning intensified.

The Invasion Begins

In preparation for D day, U.S. troops begin to unload massive amounts of military supplies.

The Allies would land six divisions of infantrymen at five connected beaches on the Normandy coast on June 6. Americans took the beaches code-named Utah and Omaha; the British, Gold and Sword; the Canadians, Juno. Supporting them were massive bombardments from the air and from naval vessels offshore, as well as the first night paratrooper landings in history.

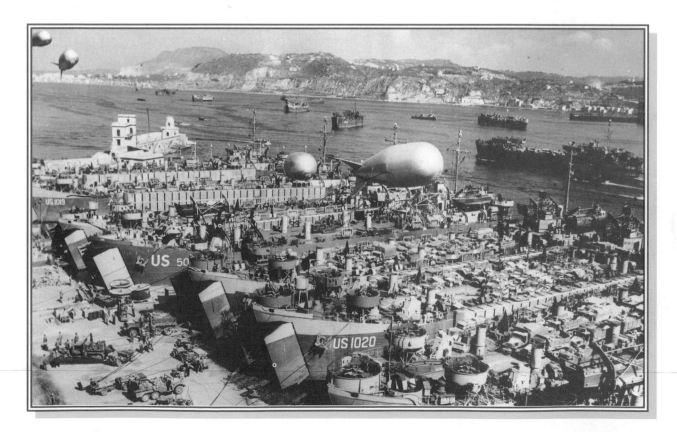

The landing at Utah Beach was comparatively uneventful; more action greeted the British and Canadians on Gold, Sword, and Juno Beaches. But those unlucky enough to land at Omaha Beach faced truly fierce German resistance. At times while the battle raged there, both German and Allied commanders thought that the Americans would end up being thrown off "Bloody Omaha."

By nightfall on D day 150,000 Allied soldiers had landed on French soil. By July 1, one million Allied troops were ashore in France. SHAEF (Supreme Headquarters Allied Expeditionary Force), the Allied high command, confidentially predicted very heavy casualties for the invasion: 10,000 dead in the initial assault. British prime minister Winston Churchill thought 20,000 would perish. The actual Allied totals were mercifully much smaller: 2,500 dead, with total losses including wounded, missing in action, and prisoners of 11,500 (6,500 Americans, 3,500 British, and 950 Canadians). No one is quite sure how many Germans died on D day; the estimates range from 4,000 to 8,000. And the heavy but very inaccurate Allied air bombardment that preceded the landings killed as many as 14,000 French civilians as well. The city of Caen was virtually destroyed.

More died as the fight for Normandy continued. By August 22, when fighting in the region ended, 210,000 Allied soldiers were casualties—37,000 dead, 154,000 wounded, and 19,200 missing. During this period some 114,000 Germans were killed.

The Price of Victory

As in every great battle, the story of D day includes numerous instances of individual bravery and heroism. Some stories are even amusing, as very nervous men, often just out of high school, battled their fears and managed to laugh in the face of death.

But there is nothing funny about war as a whole. It is a stupid, ugly, and grotesque exercise, exacting a terrible price in human blood and sacrifice. Each casualty on D day had a name, a face, friends and family. Death was not clean and neat. Some were blown to pieces. Others burned alive in American tanks or German concrete pillboxes. Arms and legs were blown away, faces unrecognizably smashed. Some of the thousands wounded remain in the veterans hospitals of both sides a half century later.

Sometimes nations have little choice but to fight; soldiers must march and sometimes die because the alternative to fighting is slavery or tyranny. Normandy was such a time, and those who waded ashore to liberate Europe from Nazism paid such a price.

We are still in their debt.

An American medical officer bandages the hand of a soldier who was injured during the invasion of Normandy.

CHAPTER ONE

Hitler's War

The roots of the Second World War lie in the ending of the First World War. For most of World War I, Kaiser Wilhelm I's Germany seemed on the verge of victory. Imperial armies had conquered great stretches of Russian, Belgian, and French territory. In 1917 czarist Russia collapsed, and the Bolshevik government that ultimately took control begged for peace with Germany. Victory seemed around the corner.

But before the Germans could bring their resources to bear on crushing France and Britain their fortunes turned. In April 1917 the United States declared war on Germany, and fresh American troops strengthened the struggling Allied Western Front. Germany's allies—Austria-Hungary, Bulgaria, and Turkey—collapsed. By November 1918 Kaiser Wilhelm abdicated, the monarchy ended, and Germany sued for peace.

The Stab in the Back

Many Germans could not believe what had happened. Victory had seemed within their grasp. Only some sort of treason, a "stab in the back," they rationalized, could have caused the German fatherland's defeat and disgrace. Many looked for scapegoats. They blamed Jews, Socialists, and Bolsheviks for Germany's downfall.

Adding to Germans' resentments were the terms of the Treaty of Versailles, the agreement that ended the war. President Woodrow Wilson's "Fourteen Points" had promised "self-determination of nations," meaning populations could form new nation-states to belong to. Poland, Czechoslovakia, Hungary, Lithuania, Latvia, Estonia, and Finland were created as a result. But the Allies set out to render the new Germany weak politically and militarily. Ethnic Germans in Poland, the Free City of Danzig, and the Sudeten region of Czechoslovakia could not join the new republic of Germany. German-speaking Austria was specifically forbidden to join with Germany. The new German republic was also saddled with huge reparation payments. Under a "war guilt clause," the nation had to accept complete responsibility for the outbreak of World War I. In addition, all German colonies in Africa and Asia were seized. German regions such as Alsace-Lorraine were partitioned off to other nations. A particularly galling condition was the physical separation of the province of East Prussia from the rest of Germany, creating a "Polish Corridor" that gave Poland access to the Baltic Sea. Also, German military troop levels were severely limited, and a German air force was forbidden altogether.

An Allied naval blockade continued even after the war ended, and widespread German starvation and hardship resulted when food and supplies could not reach the devastated and defeated people. In the early 1920s hyperinflation, very high rates of inflation over a very short time, wrecked the German economy and eliminated many people's life savings. The worldwide Great Depression of the 1930s hit Germany particularly hard. Yet Germany was still saddled with huge reparation payments that its poor economy could not possibly hope to meet. Germans were ready for radical change.

The seeds of World War II were sown at the signing of the Treaty of Versailles. The humiliating terms dictated by the treaty left Germany smoldering for revenge.

Several political parties flourished in Germany to cater to these attitudes. The Nationalists proposed restoring the German kaiser and central government to alleviate Germany's problems. A strong Communist Party also flourished. And then the National Socialists, or Nazis, also offered a solution.

The Nazis have been described as a combination of the medieval and the super-modern. In many ways their program was like that of the Nationalists—authoritarian, traditional in taste, and militaristic. Yet they took the "Socialist" in their name very seriously. They called for a leveling of class distinctions and for placing the national good above that of the individual. To all of this the Nazis added a litany of violent resentments—against those diplomats who "lost" the war, against Communists, against Jews, against Marxian Socialists, against neighboring Slavs such as the Poles and Russians. The Nazis preached doctrines of racial purity, German superiority, and anti-Semitism that would eventually lead to the Holocaust, the systematic murder of ten million Europeans, six million of whom were Jews.

Der Führer

The Nazis' leader was an impassioned orator named Adolf Hitler. Despite his charismatic speaking skills Hitler was an unlikely candidate for German leadership. Born in Austria in 1889, he did not become a German citizen until February 1932. His early life was marked by failure. The young Hitler fancied himself a painter, but

Adolf Hitler, leader of the Nazi Party, rose to power on a platform that included a systematic form of German nationalism called Aryanism. He advocated a program of eliminating Jews, which capitalized on the resentment the Germans already felt toward them. At right, a German textbook explains the inherent superiority of Germans over Jews.

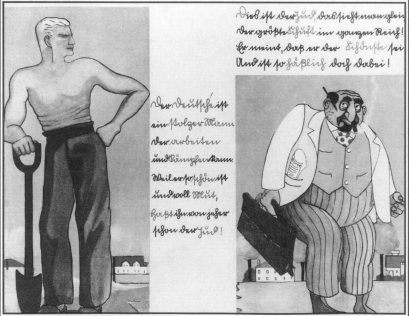

was refused entrance to Vienna's Academy of Fine Arts, and lived there in flophouses and men's hostels, virtually a derelict.

In 1913 Hitler was about to be drafted into the Austro-Hungarian army, but he had little desire to serve a government he believed betrayed German interests by catering to Slavs and Jews. He moved to the Bavarian city of Munich in southern Germany, and when World War I broke out in 1914 he enthusiastically enlisted in the Bavarian infantry. Millions died in the four years of World War I, but Hitler developed a strange sense of purpose and happiness amidst the widespread death and destruction.

After the war Hitler remained in the army. His superiors ordered him to spy on a small radical group, the German Workers Party. Hitler saw possibilities in the tiny organization, left the army, and soon became the party's leader, or führer. In 1923 he led an unsuccessful coup or putsch against the fledgling German republic. It was a total disaster. Hitler was arrested but skillfully used his trial as a forum to attack the established order. He served less than a year of a five-year prison sentence, during which time he wrote *Mein Kampf* ("my struggle"), outlining his racist, anti-Semitic plans for world domination. In the years following his release Hitler and his party, now called National Socialists, steadily increased their popular and political support.

In January 1933 Hitler was named chancellor of Germany. On the death of aged German president Paul von Hindenburg, he assumed that office as well and consolidated it with the chancellorship. Hitler became the all powerful führer of what he called the Third Reich (i.e., the third unified German state: the first was the Holy Roman Empire; the second was Imperial Germany under Kaiser Wilhelm) and eventually exercised almost total control over German life.

In the 1930s Hitler enjoyed a string of successes that raised his popularity to unheard-of levels. The German economy improved. Unemployment dropped. In defiance of the Treaty of Versailles, Hitler stationed German troops in forbidden areas of Germany. Hitler also joined Austria and Germany through a forced union or *Anschluss*, again defying the treaty. The region of 3.5 million German-speakers in the Czech Sudetenland was incorporated into Germany as well. To the average German, Hitler was restoring pride to Germany by refusing to kowtow to the unfair restrictions placed on it.

Peace in Our Time

All of Hitler's accomplishments had been achieved through largely peaceful means, although threats of force and war were never very far away. Many in the West felt that Hitler's blustery demands were not baseless and that he could be appeased by granting him concessions.

Appeasement at Munich

At the 1938 Munich Conference the policy of appeasing Adolf Hitler reached its peak. Intending to seize the largely German Sudetenland Hitler had long encouraged the three million Sudeten Germans to oppose the Slavic Czech government. Fired by his hatred of all Slavs, Hitler's ultimate aim was the destruction of the Czech state.

Neither Britain nor France wanted to fight Hitler. When in September 1938 it appeared Hitler might invade Czechoslovakia to achieve his aims, the leaders of Britain and France, Neville Chamberlain and Eduard Daladier, were all too eager to trade the Sudetenland for Hitler's assurances of peace. They believed this would satisfy Hitler's appetite for European territory.

Chamberlain promised to hold an international conference on the Sudetenland issue. Hitler, Chamberlain, Daladier, and Italian Fascist dictator Benito Mussolini gathered in Munich to decide Czechoslovakia's fate. No Czech leader was invited to attend. Within twelve hours Chamberlain and Daladier gave away the Sudetenland. When Chamberlain returned to London he announced that he had brought home "peace in our time . . . peace with honor."

Hitler thought differently. "My enemies were worms," he once observed. "I saw them at Munich."

That changed in March 1939 when, after partitioning the Sudetenland, Hitler seized much of the rest of Czechoslovakia, breaking his promise that "the Sudetenland is the last territorial demand I have to make in Europe." No longer gullible Westerners realized that Hitler's promises were worthless and that he had to be stopped.

Although the West finally began to exercise caution with Hitler, Soviet dictator Joseph Stalin saw an opportunity to capitalize on Hitler's progress. In August 1939 National Socialist Germany and the Communist Soviet Union, previously bitter enemies, signed a nonaggression pact, under which Germany and the USSR would divide Poland while the Soviet Union would annex Lithuania, Latvia, Estonia, and the Romanian province of Bessarabia. The agreement allowed Hitler to wage war without fear of fighting strong enemies on two fronts.

The Germans invade Poland in a rapid blitzkrieg. *The invasion would be a mere prelude to greater German aggression.*

On the morning of September 1, 1939, Hitler's *Wehrmacht* (army) and *Luftwaffe* (air force) launched a *blitzkrieg* ("lightning war") into Poland. On September 17 the Soviet Red Army attacked from the east. By September 20 Polish resistance had virtually ceased. On September 3 France and the United Kingdom declared war on Germany; World War II had begun.

After Poland fell, the winter of 1939–1940 was oddly quiet. This inactivity in central Europe was dubbed the *sitzkrieg*, or "phony war." There was, however, other military activity. In November the Soviet Union attacked Finland. Outnumbered five to one, the Finns fought back valiantly, ultimately maintaining their independence although ceding territory to Stalin.

The Russo-Finnish War focused attention on northern Europe. Britain and France pondered action in Norway to help the Finns. Germany, however, struck first. In April 1940 the Nazis invaded both Denmark and Norway. Denmark surrendered immediately; Norway put up a brief fight but was soon conquered.

In the spring of 1940 Hitler turned his blitzkrieg on France. Hitler repeated the tactics used in World War I by attempting to end-run French defenses,

invading through Belgium and violating its neutrality. But he added an important new strategic dimension: an armored thrust through the Ardennes forest. The Ardennes represented a major gap in France's defense; the French simply did not believe that an armored attack through the densely wooded Ardennes could succeed.

They were wrong. In May 1940 Hitler's *panzers* (tanks) hurtled through the Ardennes, routing French and British troops. By May 26 Anglo-French forces had retreated into a pocket centered on the English Channel port of Dunkirk. Miraculously, a ragtag flotilla of 850 British vessels evacuated 338,226 soldiers from Dunkirk, saving a major Allied defeat from devastating losses and boosting Allied morale.

British and French forces await evacuation at Dunkirk. Remarkably, the evacuation was accomplished by a ragtag assembly of civilian boats and ships.

"Blood, Toil, Tears, and Sweat"

Also adding to British spirit was new leadership. Prime Minister Neville Chamberlain, an advocate of appeasement (granting concessions to Hitler to maintain the peace), was replaced by Winston Churchill, a longtime advocate of stern measures against Hitler. Although he claimed to offer Britons nothing but "blood, toil, tears, and sweat," Churchill rallied his fellow citizens from their despair after a string of military defeats.

On June 9 Germany's Fascist ally, Italy, declared war on France. German troops were marching toward Paris; the French government fell apart. Marshal Philippe Pétain, a hero of World

Churchill: The Lion Roars

Winston Churchill had been a prominent—if somewhat erratic—British public figure since the turn of the century. In World War I, as First Lord of the Admiralty (head of the British Royal Navy) he led the Allied amphibious invasion of Germany's ally Turkey at Gallipoli, an operation that was a massive Allied disaster. After 1929 his political career went into eclipse; he held no public office and supported himself as a journalist.

As early as 1930, however, Churchill warned his countrymen of the dangers of Nazism. Throughout the decade he attacked Neville Chamberlain's policy of appeasement. But such warnings only made Churchill more unpopular in a nation determined to avoid another war at almost any cost. Historian John Lukacs in *The Duel* accurately describes the Churchill of the 1930s as "a discredited politician, shunned and distrusted by a majority of his own political party [the Conservatives], the ruling party in Britain."

When war came, however, Chamberlain reappointed Churchill First Lord of the Admiralty. Again Churchill oversaw a major Allied loss, as Hitler bested the British navy in Norway. But when France fell, so did Chamberlain's government. Because Churchill had long and loudly opposed Hitler, he was chosen to replace Chamberlain.

The outlook was bleak, but Churchill used his oratorical skills to rally Britons and to restore the nation's morale. Churchill told his fellow citizens they must not waver:

> What [French] General Weygand called the Battle of France is over. The Battle of Britain is about to begin. . . . The whole fury and might of the enemy must very soon be turned upon us. Hitler knows he must break us in this island or lose the war. . . .
>
> If we fail, then the whole world, including the United States, including all that we have known and cared for, will sink into the abyss of a new Dark Age, made more sinister, and perhaps more protracted, by the lights of perverted science.
>
> Let us therefore brace ourselves to our duties, and so bear ourselves that if the British Empire and its Commonwealth last for a thousand years, men will still say, "This was their finest hour."

Churchill's wartime rhetoric and leadership indeed helped make this Britain's finest hour, although it is doubtful the United Kingdom could have defeated Hitler without the aid of the Soviet Union and the United States. Nevertheless, it was Churchill who best articulated the unwavering resolve of those who opposed Nazism's horrors.

However, as the war ended, British voters turned away from Churchill's leadership. They had had enough of "blood, toil, tears, and sweat." Britons wanted security and voted Churchill's Conservatives out of power. Winston Churchill, victorious in war, was one of peacetime's first casualties, losing the 1945 general elections to the socialist Labor Party and forced from office.

Winston Churchill led the British people to eventual victory with inspiring speeches and astute leadership.

War I, assumed the premiership and quickly negotiated an armistice with the Nazis. The Germans occupied Paris on June 14 but allowed Pétain to form a new government in the central commune of Vichy and to rule over southeastern France.

It was widely expected that Hitler would next invade Britain. Lacking significant naval forces, in August 1940 Germany launched an air attack instead, known thereafter as the Battle of Britain. In September German bombers struck at London, and for 57 consecutive nights an average of 400 *Luftwaffe* planes (including 160 bombers) pounded London. Although the British were outnumbered, they eventually triumphed. By the time Nazi bombing of the United Kingdom stopped two years later, the *Luftwaffe* had lost 1,733 aircraft, compared to just 915 downed British planes.

Buildings crumble in ruins around the shadow of St. Paul's Cathedral in London. The Germans attempted to subdue the British with massive air strikes and firebombs.

Operation Barbarossa

As German fighters were taking a beating in the skies over England, Hitler was already turning his attention eastward, to the lebensraum he had long coveted for Germans from the Soviet Union. Even before the Battle of Britain, Hitler ordered his generals to prepare for the conquest of the Soviet Union, codenamed Operation Barbarossa.

Hitler originally wanted to invade the USSR in the fall of 1940, but his generals persuaded him not to, warning of the harsh Russian winter. Then in 1941 Hitler's revised plans were sidetracked when his Italian Axis ally, Benito Mussolini, became a major liability.

Frustrated by his failure to play a major role in the invasion of France (his armies stalled a few miles after crossing the border), Mussolini sought to imitate Hitler's military victories, and from Albania (conquered by Italy in April 1939) he invaded Greece on October 28, 1940. His armies were stopped by the British, who gained a new foothold on the European continent.

Hitler could not allow Britain to station planes within striking distance of the Ploesti oil fields in Romania, which would be his main source of petroleum once he invaded the Soviet Union. He also could not allow his ally and friend Mussolini to fail so miserably.

So, on April 6, 1941, Hitler invaded Greece, but to do so he had to send his troops across Yugoslavia. This was a problem; although Hungary, Romania, and Bulgaria had become German partners, Yugoslavia had not. The Third Reich thus had to invade both Greece *and* Yugoslavia. The operation was a success but cost Hitler precious time in his schedule for Operation Barbarossa. Greek and Allied forces held out on the island of Crete until late May when the Germans launched history's first successful airborne invasion, landing thousands of paratroopers on Crete from *Luftwaffe* planes.

World War II, 1939–1942

Meanwhile, Mussolini's armies in North Africa also found themselves in trouble and in February 1941 Hitler created the Afrika Korps, two tank divisions under General Erwin Rommel. The corps was to prop up the Italians and prevent Libya from falling to Britain.

Hitler's Soviet invasion was therefore pushed back from the spring of 1941 to that summer. On June 22, 1941, 3 million German, Italian, Hungarian, Bulgarian, Romanian, and Finnish troops, a total of 121 divisions, invaded the USSR. Despite numerous warnings, Stalin was caught by surprise. Adding to Soviet problems was Stalin's wholesale purge of his officer corps in the late 1930s, which stripped the Red Army of experienced leadership. Stalin stubbornly and unwisely refused to allow his commanders to retreat from the German onslaught. Whole armies were easily surrounded by fast-moving panzer units. In the first two days of the invasion 2,000 Soviet aircraft were destroyed. In the first 18 days, the Germans advanced 400 miles, capturing 300,000 prisoners, 1,000 tanks, and 600 aircraft. By July 10 the *Wehrmacht* was within 10 miles of Leningrad; in mid-July they stood within 200 miles of Moscow. By September more than 1 million Soviet soldiers had fallen prisoner to the German armies.

The German Center Army entered the Moscow suburbs in early December 1941, but Red Army resistance had been stiffening since the fall, and on December 6 Soviet general Georgy Zhukov counterattacked, sending the Germans into a forty-mile retreat. They would never again be so close to Moscow.

Enter the United States

On December 7, 1941, an event occurred that changed the course of the war: Japan attacked Pearl Harbor, America's large naval base in Hawaii. The United States had officially been a neutral party in the war till then, although its sympathies (and some of its actions,

The bombing of Pearl Harbor by the Japanese quickly did what all of Churchill's pleading could not do—get the United States involved in the war against Hitler.

Nazi soldiers send coded messages with an Enigma.

The ULTRA Secret

The ultimate prize in military intelligence is access to enemy communications. The British won this prize in World War II. Before war erupted the Germans devised an incredibly advanced encryption or coding device called Enigma. The Enigma machine looked like a small typewriter but, fitted out with special cylinders and electronic circuits, it devised almost unbreakable codes on a daily, and later hourly, basis.

Almost unbreakable. In 1939 anti-Nazi activists smuggled an Enigma machine out of Germany and gave it to the British, who assembled a team of cryptographers to crack the code. By 1942 they succeeded and from then on knew almost immediately of top secret German decisions and actions. This was the secret codenamed ULTRA, for if the Nazis once learned their opponents had this capability they would stop using Enigma and the Allied advantage would be lost. In fact, ULTRA was so secret it was not revealed to the public until 1974.

Having this inside knowledge of Hitler's plans would prove invaluable in plotting an invasion of France.

General Bernard "Monty" Montgomery's Eighth Army halted the advance of Erwin Rommel's Afrika Korps at El Alamein in North Africa.

such as lend-lease aid to Britain) clearly favored the Allies. President Franklin D. Roosevelt proclaimed December 7 "a day that will live in infamy" and the United States declared war on Japan, which joined Germany and Italy in the Axis alliance. On December 11 Hitler declared war on the United States. Soon American GIs would be actively aiding the Allied war effort.

In Europe the war on the eastern front continued. The Germans were unprepared for the bitter cold of Russian winters and suffered terribly, but the next spring went on the offensive again. By the fall of 1942 the German Sixth Army, under General Friedrich von Paulus, reached Stalingrad in southern Russia. But by February 1943 the Sixth Army had been destroyed. Ninety thousand Germans were taken prisoner; three hundred thousand Germans were killed or wounded.

In North Africa, Erwin Rommel, with only limited resources at his disposal, had turned the situation completely around for the Axis powers and invaded British-held Egypt. He advanced as far as El Alamein before being halted by British general Bernard Montgomery's Eighth Army. Rommel advanced no further: In November 1942 Operation Torch saw American and British forces land in Vichy-held Morocco and Algeria, and by May 1943 the Allies were in total control of North Africa.

Early in July 1943 British and American forces struck again, landing on the Italian island of Sicily. In late July Mussolini resigned, and in September the Allies invaded the Italian mainland. The new Italian government quickly surrendered, but German forces in Italy fought back fiercely. Allied forces landed at Anzio, just south of Rome, in January 1944 and Rome fell to the Allied armies on June 4, 1944.

The Germans were being forced back all along the eastern front. They had been ousted from North Africa and Sicily and were steadily being pushed up the Italian peninsula. One giant step in the Allied strategy had yet to be accomplished, however: the invasion and liberation of France.

CHAPTER TWO

Fortress Europe

At its peak, Hitler's empire stretched from France's Spanish border to the gates of Leningrad and Stalingrad. Until he suffered severe reversals at Stalingrad and El Alamein in late 1942, Hitler's advances were rapid and relentless. Defending his gains was not a priority. But as one defeat followed another, as American troops reached Britain in ever-increasing numbers and as his *Luftwaffe* vanished from the skies, the need to establish a strong defensive line around his conquests became increasingly important.

To that end Hitler established a much vaunted "Atlantic Wall" of modern fortifications along the west coast of Europe, designed to protect what he called *Festung Europa* ("Fortress Europe"). It would comprise 15,000 strongholds (centered by artillery emplacements and machine-gun and mortar nests) to be held by 300,000 men.

After the Allies' successful amphibious invasions of North Africa, Sicily, and the Italian mainland, it was obvious that their next goal would be to liberate occupied France. As 1944 progressed it was clear the Allies were preparing to test Hitler's Atlantic Wall.

Vichy France: Collaboration in Action

France had quickly collapsed in 1940. Marshal Philippe Pétain's policy of collaboration with the Nazis made France a virtual ally of its former enemy. Although Vichy never formally entered the war on the Nazi side, it actively persecuted its Jewish population and eagerly cooperated economically with Germany.

Hitler stands smugly before France's Eiffel Tower in June 1940. At the time, Hitler's rapid invasions were virtually unopposable.

To boost France's economy (one million citizens were unemployed in 1940) Vichy leaders did not hesitate to aid Hitler's war effort against Britain. Author Werner Rings, in his book *Life with the Enemy: Collaboration and Resistance in Hitler's Europe*, contends, "Moves toward economic cooperation emanated more from the vanquished than the victor. Putting it more strongly, one would have to say the French flung themselves at the Germans."

Yet even that did not satisfy Hitler, who cruelly exploited every nation in conquered Europe. Reich minister of propaganda Joseph Goebbels wrote in his diaries: "If the French knew what demands the Führer will one day make on them, their eyes would probably pop. That's why it's better to keep mum about such things for the present." Goebbels knew Hitler was planning extensive looting of the French economy and more repression of French civil liberties.

Officially, Pétain remained in office, but in April 1942 Pierre Laval became Vichy's chief of government and shortly thereafter publicly affirmed his desire for a German victory. That November the Germans boldly occupied the rest of France. Pétain and Laval retained their offices but were now without question German puppets.

A Defensive Strategy

With Hitler's forces directed at the unsuccessful invasion of the Soviet Union in the fall of 1942, he realized that his western flank, particularly in France, was dangerously exposed to Allied invasion. He correctly surmised it would be necessary for the Germans to destroy any Allied landing force before reinforcements could be landed. However, as did Stalin on the eastern front, he stubbornly forbade any retreat, even a purely tactical one. Such inflexible strategy would make any German defensive posture that much more vulnerable after an enemy landing.

On March 23, 1942, he issued the following order:

In the days to come the coasts of Europe will be seriously exposed to the danger of enemy landings. . . .

All available forces and equipment of the several services . . . will be committed by the responsible commander for the destruction of enemy transport facilities and invasion forces. That commitment must lead to the collapse of the enemy attack, before, if possible, but at the latest upon the actual landing.

An immediate counterattack must annihilate landed enemy forces, or throw them back in the sea. All instruments of warfare are to be jointly committed toward that end.

No headquarters and no unit may initiate a retrograde movement in such a situation.

In June 1944 Germany had approximately 60 divisions (1,400,451 men), about one-quarter of its entire army, in France. Thirty-six infantry divisions and 6 armored divisions were arrayed along the northern French coast, guarding against Allied landings.

Most German generals felt an invasion would take place in the Pas de Calais region, just across the English Channel from Britain and the most attractive landing site for Allied planners. Accordingly, two and a half times as many German troops and heavy guns were stationed there than in Normandy, the peninsula to the southwest.

Just three German divisions held Normandy. The 709th defended the north and east coast. The 243rd was on the west coast, and the 91st—recently arrived in the area—held the peninsula's inland position. Just beyond Normandy was another unit, Baron von der Heydte's tough 6th Parachute Regiment, a battle-hardened paratroop unit. A total of nearly forty thousand Germans waited in and around Normandy for an Allied attack, but with some exceptions (such as von der Heydte's troops) they were not crack units. Many were Poles, Russians, or other East Europeans forced into the German military. Others were older Germans, in the army only because the Reich had exhausted its supply of younger men. By May 1944, one-third of all German soldiers were over thirty-four years of age.

An Inadequate Navy

Except for submarine warfare, naval strategy was never a German strength, and by 1944 the *Kriegsmarine*, the German navy, had been badly battered from years of British and American attack.

German submarines known as U-boats line a German harbor. The German navy was Hitler's weak spot.

Guarding a coastline that stretched 2,500 miles from Denmark to Spain, by May 1944 it possessed little fighting strength: 96,000 men, 11 destroyers and torpedo boats, approximately 300 mine sweepers and 116 assorted patrol vessels, and 49 U-boats or submarines. In the Normandy area the Germans had only 4 destroyers, 31 torpedo boats, and 15 U-boats. Not only was this force too small to repel an Allied invasion (on D day nearly 100,000 Allied sailors would man 5,000 ships, including 5 battleships, 23 cruisers, 105 destroyers, 284 escorts, 291 minesweepers and minelayers, 2,700 troopships, and 495 patrol vessels), but it was insufficient for even the relatively simple tasks of reconnaissance or weather reporting.

The Vanishing *Luftwaffe*

At one time Hitler boasted that 1,000 German planes would swoop down on any invader. As the war dragged on, and *Luftwaffe* air superiority faded, his promise proved fanciful. By early June 1944 only 183 fighter planes remained in all of France. Of these only 160 were in working order. Trying to cover both the Pas de Calais and Normandy, on June 4 the German High Command ordered the last of the *Luftwaffe*'s fighters away from the Normandy area. "This is crazy!" stormed German fighter ace Colonel Josef "Pips" Priller. "If we're expecting an invasion the squadrons should be moved up, not back! And what happens if the attack comes during the transfer? My supplies can't reach the new bases until tomorrow or maybe the day after. You're all crazy!"

And so on June 6, 1944, only two German planes were left in Normandy to repel the greatest sea invasion in history.

At the beginning of the war, the German air force, Luftwaffe, *seemed unbeatable. Before the Normandy invasion, however, Hitler's* Luftwaffe *was little more than a skeleton.*

Field Marshal von Rundstedt

As the Allies assembled men and matériel in England, it became apparent that skillful German leadership would be necessary to defeat any European landing. In 1942 Hitler appointed Field Marshal Gerd von Rundstedt as commander in chief of German forces in the west. His main responsibility was to guard against the feared Allied invasion.

The aging von Rundstedt was in some sense a relic of the old aristocratic Prussian military tradition, having first joined the German officer corps in 1893 at the age of eighteen. When war broke out in 1939 he was already in retirement. But it would be a mistake to dismiss him as a doddering antique. He led the *Wehrmacht* in the invasion of Poland as well as in the pivotal armored dash through the Ardennes that triggered France's quick collapse. He also fought skillfully in Operation Barbarossa, commanding the Southern Army Group and advancing as far as Rostov-on-Don. Faced with renewed Soviet strength there, however, he ignored orders and oversaw a highly successful tactical retreat from the city. Hitler, who never could grasp the necessity of tactical withdrawals, relieved von Rundstedt of his command in November 1941.

Von Rundstedt, whom Dwight Eisenhower would later praise as "the most accomplished soldier we met," was often contemptuous of Hitler, whose social origins and military credentials were far beneath his own. He called Hitler "that Bohemian corporal" and dismissed the Atlantic Wall as an "enormous bluff . . . more for the German people than for the enemy . . . and the enemy, through his agents, knows more about it than we do."

The field marshal had never believed in the effectiveness of fixed defensive positions. His scorn for such ideas was only strengthened by his successful end-run against France's Maginot Line. Von Rundstedt wanted to oppose any invasion by keeping German forces away from the coast and then surging forward, engaging the Allies while they were still relatively weak and disorganized, and throwing them back into the sea.

Soon, Hitler would give him an assistant who did not share those views.

The Desert Fox

That assistant was the legendary hero of Germany's Afrika Korps, General Erwin Rommel, "the Desert Fox." A soldier of such skill should have been welcomed by von Rundstedt, but the field marshal soon found Rommel and he were working at cross purposes.

After the Allies conquered North Africa and defeated the Afrika Korps, Rommel (promoted to field marshal by Hitler in June 1942) was placed in charge of Army Group B in northern

A Divided Command

Rommel's and von Rundstedt's disagreement over which defensive strategy to pursue was not the only division in the German ranks.

Hitler's Third Reich was a confusing tangle of overlapping and conflicting authority and responsibilities. Several government agencies might be entrusted with the same mission, resulting in confusion and counterproductive rivalries. Ultimately Hitler would be called on to settle disputes—reinforcing, of course, his own authority and power.

Such conflicts extended into the armed forces. The German air force, the *Luftwaffe*, stationed 337,140 men in France alone, most of whom were ground forces, including 30,000 parachute troops. In the Atlantic ports, the German navy controlled artillery, but more than 100,000 *Luftwaffe* personnel oversaw antiaircraft guns. And even though Field Marshal Rommel was acknowledged master of tank warfare, 4 tank divisions in France were under the control of General Leo Geyr von Schweppenburg's Panzer Group West.

Complicating the situation further, the 1st Waffen SS ("Armed SS") Panzer Corps, consisting of the Panzer Lehr Division, the 1st and 12th SS Panzer Divisions, and the 17th SS Panzergrenadier Division, was under the direct control of OKW, the German High Command in Berlin. No German commander (even Rommel or von Rundstedt) stationed within France could order these vital reserve armored units into battle in an emergency. Thus when an invasion actually came, precious hours would be lost in responding, a disadvantage the undermanned *Wehrmacht* could ill afford.

Italy. In December 1943 Hitler named him inspector of coastal defenses in northern France. The following month he was also given command of the German Army Group B in France, consisting of General Hans von Salmuth's Fifteenth Army near the Pas de Calais and Colonel General Friedrich Dollman's Seventh Army, defending Normandy and Britanny.

Rommel disagreed vigorously with his superior, von Rundstedt, on how to defeat an Allied attack. Rommel theorized: "The [Allied] troops are unsure and possibly even seasick [when they land]. They are unfamiliar with the terrain. Heavy weapons are not yet available in sufficient quantity. This is the moment to strike and defeat them."

Rommel had lost to the British at El Alamein primarily because his overextended supply lines, stretching for hundreds of miles across the African desert, were vulnerable to Allied air superiority. He faced the same problem in France and, unlike Von Rundstedt, doubted that the Germans would be able to quickly maneuver their forces around and overwhelm an Allied force. Rommel believed:

> The war will be won or lost on the beaches. We'll have only one chance to stop the enemy and that's while he's still in the water . . . struggling to get ashore. Reserves will never get up to the point of attack and it's foolish even to consider them. The *hauptkampflinie* [the primary line of German resistance] will be here. . . . The first twenty-four hours of the invasion will be decisive . . . for the Allies, as well as Germany, it will be the longest day.

Perhaps Rommel was right. Perhaps von Rundstedt was right. Most likely neither strategy could have halted a strong Allied landing. But in the confused German High Command no decision was ever made on which strategy to follow, and combining aspects of the two approaches almost guaranteed defeat. Said General Omar Bradley, commander of the U.S. First Army: "The result was a defensive crust at the beaches that was too thin to destroy us and reserves too small for von Rundstedt's war of maneuver."

Rommel Takes Over

Like most other Germans, Rommel had believed Nazi propaganda that the Atlantic Wall could easily repel any invasion. On inspecting it, however, he quickly discovered it was a "figment of Hitler's *Wolkenkuckucksheim* [cloud cuckoo land]." Only a few areas around several key ports were even remotely secure.

Beyond that Rommel questioned the basic concept of the Wall's structure. He felt that the existing plan, relying only on fixed bunkers and machine-gun nests, was simply not good enough. His idea was to toughen it with a line of crude but lethal anti-invasion barriers.

The Personal Rommel

Field Marshal Erwin "the Desert Fox" Rommel was the one high-ranking German who won the respect of his Allied adversaries.

Even as the war raged *Time* magazine could respectfully write of him: "His men as well as his officers, fear and look up to him. Dashing about by car and motorcycle in the forward zones of action, he sees his men and they see him. Sometimes they have to bear the lash of his wrath, but they admire him."

Rommel was all business, but unlike many other powerful Nazi officials was low-key and willing to listen to others. "Rommel talked about military matters and his experiences with people of all kinds," wrote his naval adviser, Admiral Friedrich Ruge. "He was, however, not bent on dominating a conversation and understood how to listen to others. He had a good sense of humor, even when he was the butt of a joke."

Rommel was known for his terse commands. As Admiral Ruge noted: "In Africa Rommel had never transmitted any radio orders containing more than twelve words; if necessary he sent several successively. He intended to adhere to this practice and keep his orders brief, and convey the rest personally to the commanders on the battlefield. It made leadership more difficult, but also more successful."

Rommel was a nonsmoker who rarely drank alcohol, a devoted family man who avoided off-color humor. He cared little for fancy cuisine and seemed tireless, never sleeping more than five hours a night. After his reverses in North Africa, Rommel's health deteriorated, however, and he suffered from rheumatism, high blood pressure, severe headaches, and nervous exhaustion as the war in Europe continued.

Erwin Rommel was considered a remarkable general by both the Germans and the Allies. Rommel's criticisms of Hitler's military decisions, however, especially toward the end of the war, made him unpopular with the German leader.

Dragon's Teeth and Hedgehogs

Rommel did not have sufficient troops and airpower to stop an Allied invasion on the beaches. So he relied on an ingenious—and deadly—collection of physical barriers designed to slow down exposed Allied troops long enough that they would be easy targets for German artillery, mortars, and machine guns.

The Germans planted 20 million mines along the French Atlantic coast, 4 million of which were placed in the section along the English Channel. Half of those 4 million had been placed in only the 6 months since Rommel assumed command. That was impressive, but fell far below Rommel's ambitious ultimate goal of laying 200 million mines from Denmark to Spain.

To slow down an amphibious invasion, Rommel also installed concrete antitank obstacles called "dragon's teeth," miles of barbed wire, sharp spiked metal tank traps known as "tetrahedra," and yet more jagged metal barriers called "hedgehogs" (a hedgehog is the European version of the porcupine).

Rommel also placed thousands of heavy wooden poles at sandy beach sites. Atop each pole was a Teller land mine. When the tide raised the water level above a pole, the mine could blast a large hole in the bottom of any advancing landing craft. An Allied five-hundred-ton craft could sink in just three minutes. If the supply of mines grew short, the poles could be outfitted with spikes and jagged iron sawteeth that could rip open the bottom of a boat.

In North Africa Rommel had learned the hard way about the value of land mines combined with heavy artillery as a key defensive weapon. Now he would duplicate that British strategy by placing artillery, machine-gun nests, and millions of land and sea mines along the Atlantic Wall.

Rommel also recalled the success of German paratroopers in Crete and took precautions against an airborne invasion. He flooded low-lying areas just inland from the coast and booby-trapped open fields with sharp stakes and trip wires that would set off antipersonnel mines.

In 1944 Rommel explained: "If the enemy should ever set foot on land, an attack through the minefields against the defense works sited within them will present him with a task of immense difficulty. He will have to fight his way through a zone of death in the defensive fire of the whole of our artillery. And not only on the coast. . . . Any airborne troops who attempt to penetrate to the coast from the rear will make the acquaintance of the mined zone."

Rommel knew he was racing against the clock, that the single question about an Allied invasion was not if but when. "I have only one real enemy now," he admitted, "and that is time."

The Guessing Game

Despite his flaws as a military commander, Hitler knew the value of defeating the Allies on the beaches. "If we succeed in throwing back the invasion," he once stated, "such an attempt cannot and will not be repeated within a short time. It will mean that our reserves will be set free to use in Italy and the East."

On March 20, 1944, Hitler theorized that because of the limited number of beaches suitable for landings the invasion would take place on either the Normandy or Brittany peninsulas.

At no place along our front is a landing possible except perhaps where the coast is broken by cliffs. The most suitable, and hence the most threatened areas are the two west coast peninsulas, [containing the cities of] Cherbourg [in Normandy] and Brest [in Brittany], which are very tempting and offer the best possibilities for the formation of a bridgehead, which could be systematically enlarged.

On May 2 Hitler zeroed in further, guessing the landings would come in Normandy. At this time most of his generals still felt the Allies would invade the Pas de Calais. Hitler even correctly guessed that the Allies were targeting Cherbourg as the first port to capture. He rushed three armored divisions to positions within one hour of where the landings in fact took place. Hitler usually trusted his intuition, but this time he failed to stick to it. He mistakenly withdrew these divisions inland, too far away to quickly meet and crush the assault.

As June 1944 opened, the guessing game continued, but the Germans let down their guard. The reason: weather. Unusually severe storms in the English Channel made a landing sufficiently unlikely that Admiral Theodor Krancke, German naval chief in the west, canceled his torpedo-boat patrols of the coast, and several key German commanders took advantage of the poor conditions and left Normandy temporarily. Several traveled 125 miles inland to Rennes for war games designed to increase their ability to react to Allied initiatives. The situation under discussion: an invasion of Normandy.

The most prominent absentee was Field Marshal Rommel. At 0700 on Sunday, June 3, he left his headquarters at La Roche-Guyon near Paris for his home in Germany to be with his wife, Lucie, on her birthday, Tuesday, June 6.

Two photos show Rommel's preparations against an Allied invasion. Pictured above is an antitank trap. Rommel believed it would be impossible for an Allied tank to cross these ditches filled with mines. At left are the long wooden poles topped with mines that were intended to blow holes into the bottoms of Allied landing craft. These poles were continually being carried away by the ocean, necessitating constant monitoring and replacement.

"Wound My Heart"

In January 1944 German intelligence chief Wilhelm Canaris had discovered how the Allies would inform the French underground that an invasion was imminent. A two-part coded message would be broadcast over the radio; both parts were lines from the Paul

Concrete and Camouflage

German troops defended the coast from inside a series of concrete-protected positions including bunkers and artillery emplacements. German engineers and architects carefully drafted seven hundred standard designs for these fortifications. One design could be added to another design—or several in combination—to quickly come up with a blueprint for whatever fortification was best suited to a particular coastal site. These fortifications took the form of observation towers and posts, heavy artillery emplacements, supply bunkers, personnel bunkers, and even huge refrigerated food storage bunkers.

In addition to the security and strength of tons of concrete, the Germans relied on the more subtle art of camouflage. They disguised many of their installations as harmless civilian structures, such as homes, beach houses, shops, and churches. False windows, curtains, and even people were painted on the sides of these emplacements.

The Germans also employed a camouflage material even simpler than paint—dirt. Many German batteries were buried with dirt and immediately overplanted with grass and other vegetation.

A concrete bunker used to hide a German gun battery reveals the camouflage used by the Nazis. Fortunately, this particular bunker proved destructible—it was bombed out of action by Allied flyers.

Verlaine poem *Chanson d'Automne* ("Song of Autumn"). When the second part was transmitted that meant the invasion would occur within 48 hours.

The first line (*"Les sanglots longs des violins de l'automne,"* or "The long sobs of the violins of autumn") was broadcast on June 1 and immediately intercepted by the Germans. Von Rundstedt's Paris headquarters placed the Fifteenth Army in the Pas de Calais on full alert. Inexplicably, headquarters failed to alert the Seventh Army in Normandy of this clear danger.

At 2215 on the night of June 5, Lt. Colonel Hellmuth Meyer, the Fifteenth Army's counterintelligence chief, received word from his staff that the second line (*"Blessent mon coeur d'une languer monotone,"* or "Wound my heart with a monotonous languor") of *Chanson d'Automne* had been broadcast. Meyer quickly told his commander, General Hans von Salmuth, who flashed the momentous news to von Rundstedt's headquarters (OB West), which in turn informed OKW (*Oberkommando der Wehrmacht*—the German High Command). However, once again OB West failed to warn Rommel's Army Group B. Thus the German Seventh Army, which would face the Allied invasion force in just a few hours, was never alerted.

For months, even years, the Germans had speculated on where and when the invasion would occur. Now they knew *when*, but carelessly did not inform the army that could defeat it.

A golden opportunity had been squandered.

CHAPTER THREE

Operation Overlord

After Stalingrad and El Alamein, Nazi armies could no longer be seen as invulnerable. In fact, after late 1942 Germany never again regained any offensive momentum. With their enemies growing stronger and more numerous and their losses growing heavier, the Germans could not win the war, but how the Allies would ultimately defeat them was still in doubt.

Allied landings in North Africa and Italy had proven successful, even if casualties were often high. Britain's Winston Churchill wished to continue attacking Axis power in the Mediterranean, or Europe's "soft underbelly" as he called the area, perhaps even marching up the Italian peninsula and capturing Vienna. The Americans, on the other hand, wanted to destroy Hitler by mounting a huge amphibious attack on France to establish a new fighting front. All the while Stalin, taking very heavy casualties in the east, lobbied his western Allies for greater action to relieve the pressure on him. He wanted a second front as soon as possible and was not concerned with the problems such a landing would face.

Disaster at Dieppe

Pressure for an invasion also grew from Canadian forces stationed in Britain. By 1942 Canadians had been stationed there for two and a half years and now were 150,000 strong. They were rapidly becoming demoralized from lack of action.

In March 1942 British commandos and sailors attacked a German drydock at Saint-Nazaire in France. Their goal was to hamper the movements of Germany's immense battleship the *Tirpitz*.

Although the British took heavy losses in the raid, they succeeded in their mission of keeping the *Tirpitz* from roaming the high seas.

Emboldened by this small success, Allied Combined Operations issued the following terse command: "Please raid one of these ports in sufficient strength to persuade the enemy to react as if he were faced with actual invasion."

The Canadians soon were chosen for this raid, which bore the code name Operation Jubilee. Its primary mission was to test the Allied ability to mount a large amphibious landing. But other goals also existed: to draw the weakened *Luftwaffe* into combat; capture German documents; and possibly even divert *Wehrmacht* forces from the east.

The site chosen was the French port city of Dieppe, just across the English Channel from southeast England. Right from the start, the operation faced difficulties. Dieppe's natural terrain was difficult. The Germans had built up a tough defense system of artillery, machine-gun nests, and antiaircraft guns. The Allies then created their own problems. Jubilee had no overall commander. With each segment led by separate commands, that meant key items would not be addressed. Additionally, the Allies, confident of their ability to carry the day with infantry alone, failed to soften up the Germans by any land or sea bombardment. No paratroopers were used to create confusion behind enemy lines. Perhaps, worst of all, was the bureaucracy of the plan, which ran to 199 typewritten pages. No flexibility was permitted in deviating from it.

A British soldier returns from Dieppe without a pant leg. He is one of the lucky ones— approximately three-quarters of the soldiers who landed at Dieppe lost their lives.

The raid began late in the evening of August 19, 1942, with a flotilla of 237 Royal Navy ships appearing off the Dieppe coast. Operation Jubilee planners had counted heavily on the element of surprise. Soon that advantage evaporated, as just offshore Dieppe a convoy of German cargo ships passed by its armada.

Once the Canadians landed, events became even worse. The Germans simply tore them apart. Of the 5,100 troops who actually landed 3,648 did not come back. All 27 Canadian tanks that landed ashore were destroyed. Field Marshal von Rundstedt gleefully reported: "No armed Englishman remains on the Continent," and Marshal Pétain congratulated his German allies on the "rapid clearing of French soil."

Dieppe taught the Allies several valuable lessons. Because of the defenses the Germans were able to mass in the congestion of a major city, the Allies would no longer try to seize a fixed port. They gave hard thought to whether they should have landed paratroopers behind German lines to create confusion. They learned the necessity of preliminary bombardments, the value of controlling the skies, and—above all—the need for flexibility. The British and Canadians would not make these mistakes again. "For every soldier who died at Dieppe," British general Lord Louis Mountbatten later stated, "10 were saved on D-Day."

For his part, Field Marshal von Rundstedt was smart enough to realize the Allies would learn from this disaster. "It would be an error," he noted in an official report, "to believe that the enemy will mount his next operation in the same manner. . . . Next time he will do things differently."

A Commander Is Chosen

In November and December 1943 Roosevelt, Churchill, and Stalin met at the Iranian capital of Tehran to discuss war aims and strategies. One decision coming out of the conference was who to appoint to command Operation Overlord, the code name for the Allied invasion of Europe. Many felt it would be General George C. Marshall, the U.S. Army chief of staff. Instead Marshall remained in that position and General Dwight David "Ike" Eisenhower was named to head Overlord. As President Franklin Roosevelt returned from Tehran he stopped off in North Africa at Tunis. There he met Eisenhower. As the two men rode together in the presidential limousine, Roosevelt casually turned to Eisenhower and said, "Well, Ike, you are going to command Overlord."

"Mr. President," Eisenhower responded, "I realize that such an appointment involved difficult decisions. I hope you will not be disappointed."

Roosevelt gave Eisenhower his orders: "You will enter the continent of Europe and, in conjunction with the other United Nations, undertake operations aimed at the heart of Germany and the destruction of her armed forces."

Gifts from the Führer

As the tide of war had been turning against the Germans, the massive Allied fiasco at Dieppe raised their sagging spirits. Not only had the Canadian-British expedition been mercilessly routed at a cost of thousands of Allied lives, but Dieppe's French citizens had shown no signs of supporting the invasion and rising up against their Nazi occupiers. Their actions had been guided in part by instructions from a BBC broadcast that warned them "to refrain from all action which might compromise their safety."

Adolf Hitler though saw this inactivity as a sign of "loyalty" by the local populace. To reward such behavior Hitler, not normally known for his benevolence toward conquered peoples, sent the citizens of Dieppe a gift of ten million French francs and even more generously ordered that all Dieppe residents taken prisoner of war in the *blitzkrieg* of 1940 be set free.

However, neither the Germans nor their Vichy collaborators were quite sure how many people that number included and were not about to waste time verifying whether a POW was actually from Dieppe or not. Dieppe residents determined to take advantage of the opportunity and soon flooded their German masters with requests to free friends and relatives who were not in fact from the city at all. As a result many non-Dieppe soldiers found themselves suddenly freed from German captivity.

Stalin, Roosevelt, and Churchill meet at Tehran to discuss war aims and strategies (right). It was at this conference that Roosevelt decided to pick Dwight D. Eisenhower to lead Allied troops in the invasion of Normandy.

"Ike"

As late as 1941 Eisenhower was so little known that a newspaper identified him as "Lt. Col. D.D. Ersenbeing." Of humble origins, he was born in 1890 in Abilene, Kansas, and graduated from West Point in 1915. He learned the basics of the new tank warfare in World War I and between world wars served under General Douglas MacArthur in both Washington, D.C., and the American-controlled Philippine Islands. After the United States entered World War II General Marshall asked Eisenhower to draw up a directive for the as yet unnamed commander of the new European theater of operations (ETO). As he handed the plan to Marshall, Marshall asked Eisenhower if he was "satisfied" with it. When Eisenhower indicated he was, Marshall said he was pleased "because these are the orders you're to operate under; you're in command of ETO."

In 1943 Eisenhower developed the original (but never implemented) plan for a European invasion, Operation Roundup. He then commanded the North African, Sicilian, and Italian amphibious invasions and proved popular not only with his own troops but also with his British allies, so much so that some American generals facetiously complained, "Ike is the best commander the British have."

In January 1944 Eisenhower arrived in London to take command of SHAEF (Supreme Headquarters Allied Expeditionary Force). There he appointed British general Bernard Montgomery, the hero of El Alamein, to be operational chief of the landings.

The Plan

Before Eisenhower's appointment as commander, Operation Overlord called for three divisions to land along a 25-mile stretch of coast; that was soon expanded to five divisions landing along a 50-mile (80-kilometer) distance.

Eisenhower's original schedule called for a May 1944 invasion, but the date had to be postponed because of a shortage of landing craft. The invasion could not begin on just any date, however; timing was absolutely critical. Only six days in June contained the necessary combination of low tides (a second low tide before nightfall was required for follow-up landings) and first light at sunrise for a landing. Other factors also had to be added to the complicated equation. A rising full moon was needed for the paratroopers who would land behind enemy lines. That cut the number of days in June 1944 when an invasion could take place to just three, June 5, 6, and 7. Cloud cover could be no more than 60 percent and no lower than three thousand feet so Allied planes could get a clear look at their targets. High winds would scatter any paratroop landings. "Finally," wrote Eisenhower's chief of staff General Walter Bedell Smith, "we hoped for a fair wind blowing inshore to drive the smoke and dust of battle toward the enemy."

All of these careful calculations could easily be upset by fickle weather in the English Channel, where storms were notorious for their violence and unpredictability.

Five Beaches

There would be five separate landings on the invasion's first day (D day), along a fifty-mile stretch of north-facing beaches. Americans were to land at the two westernmost beaches, code-named Utah, at the estuary of the Vire River, and Omaha. Britons were to come ashore at Asneles, the center landing site, code-named Gold, and Oistreham, code-named Sword, the easternmost beach. Canadians were to land at a section of beach between the two British landing sites, code-named Juno.

A total of thirteen divisions were to land by the second day, seventeen by the end of the third day. From there Eisenhower planned to advance to Paris, approximately 150 miles to the east, and ultimately into Germany.

A complicated series of measures would soften up the Germans before the landings: Free French underground sabotage, British and American night paratroop landings, heavy air bombardment, and finally massive naval bombardment from ships just offshore.

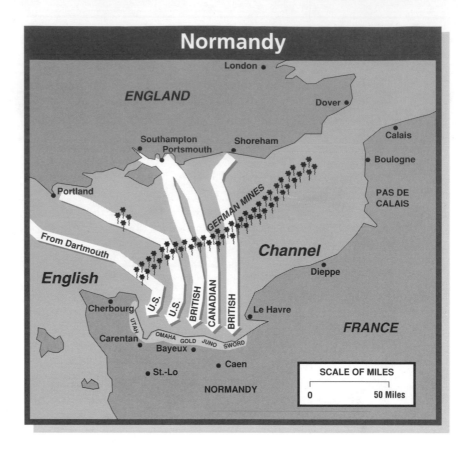

Normandy

Map labels: London, ENGLAND, Dover, Southampton, Portsmouth, Shoreham, Calais, Boulogne, PAS DE CALAIS, Portland, GERMAN MINES, Channel, From Dartmouth, English, Dieppe, Cherbourg, U.S., U.S., BRITISH, CANADIAN, BRITISH, Le Havre, FRANCE, Carentan, UTAH, OMAHA, GOLD, JUNO, SWORD, Bayeux, Caen, St.-Lo, NORMANDY

SCALE OF MILES
0 — 50 Miles

The Buildup

Assembling the men and matériel for Operation Overlord was an immense task. Eisenhower commanded an army of 3 million men: 1.7 million Americans, 1 million British and Canadians, and 300,000 representing nations still under Hitler's rule: Poles, Free French, Czechs, Norwegians, Belgians, and Dutch. All of the latter number had escaped from the mainland of Europe but were eager to return and free their homelands.

Servicing such a huge number of troops was an intimidating challenge. Chow lines a quarter-mile long were not unknown, even though there were 4,500 cooks on the American bases alone. For the invasion 163 new airbases were constructed in Great Britain. New rail lines were also laid—170 miles in all. One thousand new locomotives and 20,000 tanker and freight cars stood ready to be transported to France should the invasion prove successful.

The U.S. Services of Supply, a military support organization, eventually acquired or constructed 73.5 million square feet of storage space for invasion supplies. Those Americans responsible for ordnance (military hardware) collected 320,000 kinds of items, some as large as 10-ton wreckers. They controlled 450,000 tons of ammunition and 50,000 military vehicles.

The Phony Armies

General George S. Patton was one of World War II's most brilliant—and most controversial—generals. The colorful "Blood and Guts" Patton, who wore a pair of ivory-handled revolvers, played a key role in the North African, Sicilian, and Italian campaigns. But his career nosedived after he slapped a wounded soldier in a hospital and accused him of cowardice. A shocked public found this insensitive act outrageous. Patton was forced to apologize, and he was thereafter overlooked for any important command.

As Operation Overlord took shape, Patton found himself in yet another key role, far different from his previous ones. In one of the major deceptions in the history of warfare, a fictitious First U.S. Army Group (FUSAG or Army Group Patton), ostensibly composed of fifty divisions (one million men) stationed in southeastern England, was created.

The *Wehrmacht* had great respect for Patton, believing him to be their most clever adversary. The Germans could not fathom why the Allies would not use him in the invasion. They therefore fully believed in FUSAG's existence and predicted it would strike across the English Channel at the Pas de Calais. Their mistake would tie down their Fifteenth Army to the Pas de Calais instead of shifting it to crush the real invasion at Normandy.

Creating the illusion of such a huge force was not easy. English movie studios manufactured phony landing craft and moored them in the Thames River. At Dover a fake oil dock (a facility used to unload crucial oil supplies from oceangoing tankers) covered three square miles. All sorts of prop ammunition dumps, planes, guns, tanks, army bases, and even hospitals were constructed to fool German reconnaissance.

Creating even more confusion in Nazi minds was the equally fictitious U.S. Fourth Army, which the Nazis were led to believe was aimed at an Allied invasion of occupied Norway. As a result the Germans uselessly tied up twenty-seven more divisions in Norway.

General George S. Patton surveys his troops. Convinced that Patton would head up the invasion of France, Hitler was fooled when the U.S. took Patton out of action to head up a phony army made to look as though the Allies would strike at the Pas de Calais.

Men and equipment are loaded onto LSTs at Brixham, England. An enormous amount of men and supplies were required to carry out the landing at Normandy.

All of this made England the site of the greatest buildup of soldiers and war matériel in history. The island fairly bristled with armaments. "It was claimed rather facetiously at the time," Eisenhower later wrote, "that only the great number of barrage balloons [blimps used to hinder incoming enemy aircraft] floating constantly in British skies kept the islands from sinking under the seas [from the weight of the armaments]."

All of these figures were, of course, top secret. But even had they not been restricted, no one would have wished to talk about certain other statistics: 124,000 hospital beds to hold those who would be wounded once the fighting in France began, and thousands of coffins readied for the dead.

Port-a-Ports

After Dieppe the Allies abandoned the idea of capturing a port city. Instead they would manufacture and transport their own port facilities to make landings of men and matériel possible until actual ports could be seized.

The massive structures were code-named Mulberries (Mulberry A for the American landings and Mulberry B for the British) and consisted of an outer breakwater made of steel floats. "Their individual elements were enormous hollow structures of rein-

(Left) Troops and gear prepare to be transported to France. (Lower) The American Mulberry at Omaha Beach is unloaded off Celleville, France. The massive structures saw little action at Normandy.

forced concrete, which reminded me, when I first saw them, of nothing so much as a six-story building lying on its side," wrote American general Walter Bedell Smith. "Several such elements constituted a 'mulberry.'"

Each Mulberry was equivalent in size to the harbor of the English city of Dover. For eight months 19,000 Britons had toiled to build the Mulberries, which were towed in pieces to Normandy by 100 tugboats and then assembled.

Winston Churchill described the Mulberries as "majestic," but thirteen days after D day fierce weather destroyed Mulberry A. Mulberry B, which could harbor five hundred ships at one time,

An Unspeakable Secret

Today the death of 749 service personnel in a training exercise would be front-page news, but in the spring of 1944 that loss of life was a secret not revealed for forty years.

Secrecy was vital for Overlord's success. Any news of the disaster at Slapton Sands might prove advantageous to the Nazis, who might theorize from it that the invasion was coming at Normandy rather than in the Pas de Calais. So not only was the incident kept completely confidential, but the dead servicemen were hurriedly buried in a mass grave in the English countryside near Devon.

It was not until 1984 that Ms. Dorothy Seekings, a local resident, spoke out. "The bodies were in American uniforms," she told the press. "There were great mounds of earth in the field and I was told they were going to be buried there. I certainly never heard they were moved."

Her revelations caused a flurry of interest in Slapton Sands. The *New York Times* investigated the matter and published its findings. Military historian Edwin P. Hoyt chronicled the incident in his book *The Invasion Before Normandy: The Secret Battle of Slapton Sands*. Surprisingly, Hoyt concluded that Slapton Sands's Operation Tiger "was indeed successful beyond the dreams of its planners, because, if nothing else, it convinced all involved that they had to be 'flexible' and ready for the unexpected."

Allied soldiers imitate Normandy-like conditions during a training exercise near Devon. The training exercise would end in disaster for 749 men when German boats unexpectedly attacked the troops while they were preparing to land at the beaches.

was also severely damaged but was repaired. Although the Mulberries' time in action was brief, they were a major element in the success of Operation Overlord.

Slapton Sands

Another disaster besides Dieppe preceded D day and cast doubt on how smooth the invasion would be. On April 28, 1944, a training exercise, Operation Tiger, took place at Slapton Sands, near Devon on England's southwest coast. A massive exercise, it was designed to imitate what the Allies expected to find when they landed at Normandy's Utah beach. More than 3,000 civilians were relocated to make room for the training exercise. Eight villages and more than 180 farms were abandoned temporarily. It should not have been a disaster, but it was.

Tragedy struck when nine German E-boats (patrol boats) infiltrated the exercise and attacked two American LSTs (Landing Ships, Tank). Both LST 507 and LST 531 were sunk. Many of the men on board were ill trained and slow to abandon the sinking craft. Seven hundred and forty-nine died. All of the E-boats made it back safely to their bases in France. Despite this large loss of lives, news of the Slapton Sands disaster was suppressed to avoid damaging Allied morale.

False Alarms

Secrecy was of immense importance to the success of Operation Overlord, yet numerous breaches occurred. In March 1944 a badly wrapped envelope fell apart at Chicago's Central Post Office. Out came very official looking documents about something called Operation Overlord.

Postal authorities reported the incident to the military, who quite reasonably feared that German spies had somehow secured top secret invasion plans. Officials breathed a sigh of relief, however, when they discovered that the "culprit" was an innocent, although somewhat absentminded, German-American sergeant at SHAEF in London. He had merely misaddressed the envelope—and sent the top secret plans to his sister in Chicago.

A more public incident occurred in May 1944. Overlord planners who were careful readers of the *London Telegraph* crossword puzzle noticed answers that were top secret code words—"Overlord," "Utah," "Omaha," "Mulberry," and "Neptune," (Overlord's naval component)—appeared with suspicious frequency. Could they be signals from a German agent? Military intelligence agents questioned the puzzle's author, a high school physics teacher named Leonard Dawe. He had no idea what they were talking about, and police went away convinced the incident had merely been a fantastic coincidence.

A U.S. war poster emphasizes the necessity of keeping one's mouth shut. In spite of the military's best efforts, several major breaches in security occurred.

Four decades later, however, it was discovered that the matter had not been coincidental at all. In compiling his puzzles, Dawe asked his students to write down words at random for his use. His students had been in the vicinity of nearby American and Canadian bases and innocently overheard soldiers using the code words. One student wrote them on his list for Dawe. When Dawe found out what had actually happened he swore that student to secrecy.

On Sunday, June 4, an even more startling false alarm sounded. That evening an Associated Press teletype operator in New York, attempting to improve her typing speed, was at work on an available machine. Somehow what she typed "flashed" out worldwide across news service wires. Her practice message, which the Germans easily intercepted, read:

URGENT PRESS ASSOCIATED . . . FLASH EISENHOWER'S HQ ANNOUNCES ALLIED LANDINGS IN FRANCE.

Overlord Begins

As the ordinary troops of Operation Overlord steamed toward Normandy and the very real possibility of injury, capture, or death, Dwight Eisenhower sought to rally their spirits. This is what he told them:

Soldiers, Sailors, and Airmen of the Allied Expeditionary Force!

You are about to embark upon the Great Crusade, toward which we have striven these many months. The eyes of the world are upon you. The hopes and prayers of liberty-loving people everywhere march with you. In company with our brave Allies and brothers-in-arms on other Fronts, you will bring about the destruction of the German war machine, the elimination of Nazi tyranny over the oppressed people of Europe, and security for ourselves in a free world.

Your task will not be an easy one. Your enemy is well trained, well equipped and battle-hardened. He will fight savagely.

But this is the year 1944. Much has happened since the Nazi triumphs of 1940–41. The United Nations have inflicted upon the Germans great defeats in open battle, man-to-man. Our air offensive has seriously reduced their strength in the air and their capacity to wage war on the ground. Our Home Fronts have given us an overwhelming superiority in weapons and munitions of war, and placed at our disposal great reserves of fighting men. The tide has turned! The free men of the world are marching together to Victory!

I have full confidence in your courage, devotion to duty, and skill in battle. We will accept nothing less than full Victory!

Good luck! And let us all beseech the blessings of Almighty God upon this great and noble undertaking.

Dwight D. Eisenhower

General Eisenhower speaks to paratroopers just before the first assault in the invasion of France.

Allied security was stunned, but fortunately the Germans—detecting no activity as yet along the Atlantic beaches—interpreted the incident as either a mistake or an attempt to deceive them.

Bad Weather and Tough Decisions

On May 17, 1944, Eisenhower set the invasion date for June 5. In the final week of May the soldiers taking part in Overlord were locked into their bases, unable to communicate with the outside world. When the men finally set out from their barbed-wire-encircled bases for the invasion fleet, they assembled into immense truck and jeep convoys nearly one hundred miles long.

By June 3 all 170,000 soldiers taking part in the first landings were moved aboard Allied ships. Eisenhower was optimistic, but worsening weather conditions soon gave him cause for alarm. By 1000 ("ten hundred hours") on June 3 it was clear the weather would jeopardize Eisenhower's original plans. Eisenhower faced a dilemma: risk having his storm-tossed invasion force dashed onto the Normandy beaches or keep his armada at sea longer than planned and expose it to German intelligence.

Early on the morning of June 4 Eisenhower, hoping the weather would improve, put off the invasion until June 6. But improve it did not. After the 7th it would again be impossible to invade. What would Eisenhower decide?

He met again with his subordinates. Air Chief Marshal Sir Arthur Tedder and Air Chief Marshal Leigh-Mallory of Britain were skeptical of Allied chances for success on the 6th. But Montgomery calmly told Ike: "I would say 'Go.'"

A nervous but determined Eisenhower went.

CHAPTER FOUR

Softening Up the Enemy

Knowing German defenses along the Normandy coast were strong, Eisenhower was not about to send his men ashore without first applying a combination of tactics to weaken enemy resistance beforehand. In the hours just before the first soldier waded ashore the Allies would unleash a deadly combination of paratroop landings, sabotage by the French resistance, and air and naval bombardment—all on a grand scale.

A Waste of Bombs

Starting just after midnight on D day the Allies sent 3,467 heavy bombers and 1,646 medium bombers into action. They were supported by 5,409 fighter planes that strafed every German position they could find, particularly German radar. Seventy-four of 92 German radar installations on Normandy were knocked out in this way. The air attack had little effect, however, on the defenders of the beaches themselves.

At Utah, for example, heavy cloud cover ruined visibility. No one knew where bomb payloads landed. Sixty-seven of the 360 heavy bombers over Utah could not see anything and did not even bother to release their bombs.

Admitted General Omar Bradley: "The aerial bombardment, as at Utah Beach, was completely ineffective. Owing in part to poor flying weather, the 2.5 million pounds of bombs fell inland of Omaha Beach, killing some French civilians and many cattle, but few Germans."

Actually, fourteen thousand civilians died. City after city was leveled. One Allied soldier found the following bitter message written on the blackboard of a ruined schoolhouse: "Caen is destroyed. St.-Lo is destroyed. Avranches is destroyed. Coutances is destroyed . . . By the Liberators!"

Aerial bombardment of the other beaches was equally futile. Almost no German facilities were knocked out, but thousands of French civilians were killed by Allied bombs gone astray.

The Parachute Strategy

A key component in Eisenhower's strategy was the 23,490-man U.S. and Commonwealth parachute and glider force landing behind enemy lines in history's first night paratrooper attack.

They left England aboard 1,200 transport planes and 700 gliders. Eight hundred and twenty-two planes carried the 13,000 American paratroopers of Major General Matthew B. Ridgway's 82nd Airborne and Major General Maxwell D. Taylor's 101st Airborne Divisions.

The Allies planned several strategies to soften up German installations before Normandy. (Above) Though largely unsuccessful due to poor visibility, Allied bombers planned several strikes of key German strongholds. (Right) In addition, massive numbers of paratroopers were flown into areas throughout France.

To further confuse and distract the Germans, in the Lessay region southwest of the actual drop zone, the Allies also parachuted down hundreds of rubber human dummies. To each they attached a string of firecrackers, so that when they landed the Germans thought they were hearing small-arms fire.

Although an airborne operation was needed to help knock out key German gun emplacements and to prevent German reinforcements from rushing to the beaches to overwhelm the landings, not everyone favored the high-risk tactic, whose main purpose was to create immense confusion behind enemy lines. Some predicted 70 percent casualties for the operation. Air Chief Marshal Leigh-Mallory, for one, stated "at the present difficult time . . . I would be failing in my duty to you if I did not let you know that I am very unhappy about the U.S. airborne operations as now planned for the night of D minus 1 D-Day."

Once again Eisenhower overrode Leigh-Mallory's objections and ordered the jump as planned.

Dressed to Kill

American paratroopers were prepared for virtually any situation that might arise. In fact, they were so prepared they could barely carry everything provided for them.

The paratrooper's basic uniform consisted of a waterproof combat jacket and pants, scratchy long underwear, and combat boots. Stuffed in their large jacket pockets were such necessities

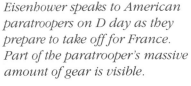

Eisenhower speaks to American paratroopers on D day as they prepare to take off for France. Part of the paratrooper's massive amount of gear is visible.

Hundreds of paratroopers descend into southern France. Although this particular maneuver was performed during the daylight hours, the initial drop at Normandy was completed at night.

as a pocketknife, extra socks, maps, a small flashlight, a razor, a spoon, and extra ammunition.

But this was just the beginning of a paratrooper's load. He also carried a Hawkins antitank mine, a Bannon Bomb, a compass, two fragmentation grenades, a .45-caliber pistol, Mae West life preserver, canteen, bayonet, first aid kit, gas mask, spare clothing, *more* ammunition, and an M-1 rifle.

The paratroopers also jumped with a three-day supply of K rations. These foul-tasting tins of provisions were hated by nearly all GIs. (More popular were D rations, which were heavy on chocolate.)

That is what the paratroopers dropped with. Once they landed they picked up even more gear. "Para-packs" of still more ammo, radios, machine guns, mortars, and medical supplies were dropped from Allied C-47s and gathered up on the ground.

"The Screaming Eagles"

General Taylor's 101st Airborne Division, "The Screaming Eagles," had two primary tasks: to capture part of the main highway from Carentan to the south of the landings (and thus badly hinder German mobility) and—more importantly—to secure the territory immediately to the rear of Utah Beach.

The enemy had flooded the area south of Utah Beach, and only a few pathways remained open through the sector. Americans landing at Utah could be hopelessly bogged down, unable to move inland and capitalize on the landing, without a secured way out.

When General Taylor parachuted in he was initially unable to make contact with more than a handful of his troops. Most of

Major General Maxwell D. Taylor headed the paratrooper invasion team known as "The Screaming Eagles." Their task was to secure the territory behind Omaha Beach.

those he found were officers; only two or three were enlisted men. "Never had so few been commanded by so many," quipped Taylor later. As dawn broke he had assembled only 1,100 of his 6,000-man contingent. Nevertheless, his men seized the German gun battery at St.-Martin-de-Varreville (although its guns had been removed) and even reached the edges of the flooded areas just behind Utah Beach.

"The All Americans"

General Matthew Ridgway's 82nd Airborne Division, "The All Americans," which landed farther inland, also had two goals. The first was to capture bridges over the Merderet and Douve Rivers, which would be vital in blocking German reinforcements from rushing to Utah Beach. The second: to capture the town of Ste.-Mere-Eglise, which stood astride the main road from Cherbourg to Carentan.

Twenty men landed in the middle of Ste.-Mere-Eglise instead of in the countryside outside the town. That was bad enough, but making their situation even worse, a building was on fire right on the square in the center of town. German soldiers accompanied local firefighters to the scene to see, much to their amazement, a handful of enemy paratroopers floating down straight at them.

The Jumping General

Leading the 82nd Airborne Division into battle was Major General Matthew Bunker Ridgway. Ridgway was no desk general. On the night of June 5–6, the forty-nine-year-old Ridgway jumped with his men in history's first night paratrooper attack.

The son of an army colonel, Ridgway graduated from West Point in 1917. In the years preceding the war he had studied the results of Soviet experimental airborne maneuvers in order to convert the 82nd from an infantry to an airborne unit. In 1941 he volunteered to make his first jump, but that did not occur until 1942—after just ten minutes of training. Ridgway was also one of the first soldiers in his 82nd Division to ride in a new type of glider. His landing was marred when the plane came down too fast. About to crash into a bomber parked on the runway, the glider was still traveling at 20 mph when Ridgway rolled out of it. Battered and bruised, he survived to jump again.

In Sicily in July 1943 Ridgway led the 82nd in the first major paratrooper attack in U.S. military history. He later commanded them on the Italian mainland. Following Normandy he oversaw operations in Belgium, the Netherlands, and Germany. In April 1951, Ridgway replaced General Douglas MacArthur as leader of UN forces in Korea.

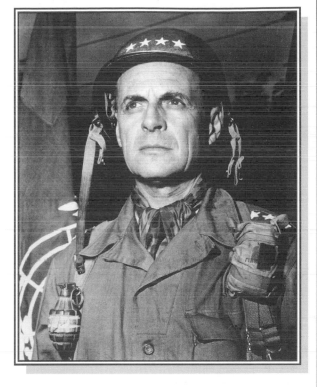

General Matthew Ridgway, the jumping general.

The last survivor of World War II's leading commanders, Ridgway died in July 1993 at age ninety-eight.

Two paratroopers fell right into the burning building, literally exploding when their explosives caught fire. Others, trapped in the branches of trees, were shot to pieces by the Germans.

Private John Steele was caught by his parachute lines in the steeple of the local church. Attempting to cut himself free, he dropped his parachute knife. His only remaining option was to pretend he was dead. So for more than two and a half hours he swung back and forth, feigning lifelessness. Finally the Germans cut him down and took him prisoner.

Ridgway and his assistant, General "Jumpin' Jim" Gavin (named because of his own skill in parachuting), gathered a few hundred men and marched toward the Merderet and Douve bridges. When they got there, they found German troops had already arrived; numerous skirmishes ensued.

After finishing off the Americans who had unluckily blown into town earlier, most Germans calmly went back to sleep. But more Americans were on their way. Realizing that in the dark they would be unable to tell friend from foe, they used an imaginative strategy: they would rely only on their knives, bayonets, and hand grenades, weapons that would not fire a flash in the dark. If the GIs saw a flash come from the barrel of a pistol or rifle they would know it came from a German weapon, and would be prepared to lob a hand grenade or attack with a knife in that direction.

The 82nd Airborne now attacked Ste.-Mere-Eglise in earnest. They quickly overwhelmed the defending German garrison. Ste.-Mere-Eglise, the first French town liberated in the war, fell at 0430 June 6.

Prior to the jump, the 82nd Airborne's Lt. Colonel Edward Krause had shown his men an American flag his previous unit (the 505th Parachute Regiment) had raised over Naples and

(Left) General "Jumpin' Jim" Gavin assisted Ridgway in marching toward Mederet and Douve bridges to destroy them. (Below) Troops relax after the initial capture of Ste.-Mere-Eglise. Little do they realize that it will take fierce fighting to hold the position.

promised that "before dawn of D day this flag will fly over Ste.-Mere-Eglise." Now, he pulled it from his pocket, marched to the village's town hall, and ran it up the flagpole.

It would be a mistake, however, to think that after the capture of Ste.-Mere-Eglise Ridgway's forces had completed their mission. Ridgway, who could only muster 40 percent of his infantry strength and 10 percent of his artillery, was soon set upon by German counterattacks. All through the night he fended off the *Wehrmacht*, who at one point were stopped just 400 yards from his command post. For 26 hours Ridgway was out of contact with the outside world. As the sun rose on June 7 his men were almost out of ammunition, but during the day more infantry and supplies arrived on gliders. By noon he was able to link up with the rapidly expanding American bridgehead on Utah Beach.

The British 6th Airborne

One of the objectives of the British 6th Airborne Division was to capture intact the bridge over the Caen Canal near the hamlet of Benouville, six miles northeast of Caen. Six gliders, carrying 180 men, would have to land in a fairly restricted area. They might have parachuted in, but coming in by glider kept all the men together on landing, as opposed to having to spend precious time regrouping after a jump.

To the west of the bridge lay Benouville itself; to the east was the river and terrain that was either marshy or very rough. The German 736th Grenadier Regiment defended the area; thirty miles to the south was the 12th SS Panzer Division, while the 21st Panzer Division had just been transferred to positions to the south and east of Caen. The bridge would have to be seized and held to prevent the panzers from crushing the landings that were soon to come.

The 6th Airborne's gliders were to be towed by Halifax bombers from Dorset in southern England and released at six thousand feet, floating silently to the ground from there. The gliders, sometimes called "flying coffins," were made of plywood and cloth and were pretty much destroyed after one landing. "What we were most afraid of was being hit by ack-ack [antiaircraft fire] or by bullets which could set us on fire," recalled Staff Sergeant Peter Boyle.

The men aboard the gliders were ready for just about anything. "We had been so well trained," said Boyle. "We did many takeoffs and landings, by day and by night, and in daytime we wore dark glasses to make it seem like night." They had to be prepared. Boyle's glider went off course and was heading for a forest. Pilot Geoff Barkway swerved the craft to the right to avoid the trees and ditched the glider in a small pond.

*British and Canadian para-
troopers move toward their
respective positions. Ultimately,
the paratroopers' goal was to
try to sabotage forces behind
the beaches and then to aid, in
any way they could, the troops
that would land at Normandy.*

The soldiers quickly overwhelmed the bridge's German guards. Barkway was one of the casualties. Recalled Boyle:

I heard Geoff shouting. He'd been shot in the wrist and had to have his right arm amputated, which put him out of the war.

We carried the wounded to the doctor, who had been in our glider and was trying to cope, although he was badly concussed in the landing. Most of the glider pilots were injured and I was bruised, but all the pilots survived the war.

The official record of the engagement stated that the mission "was carried out at the double, with the greatest dash and without pause." Unfortunately, the landing and taking of the bridge was not the end to the casualties. One hundred and four of the 6th Airborne's 180 men would be dead or wounded by day's end.

The Merville Battery

Near the village of Merville, the Germans had constructed a four-gun battery, positioned in such a way that anyone attempting to land at Sword Beach would be cut to pieces.

To give the men landing there a fighting chance, the Merville battery would have to be destroyed, but that was no easy task. Blowing it up from the air was virtually impossible, although the

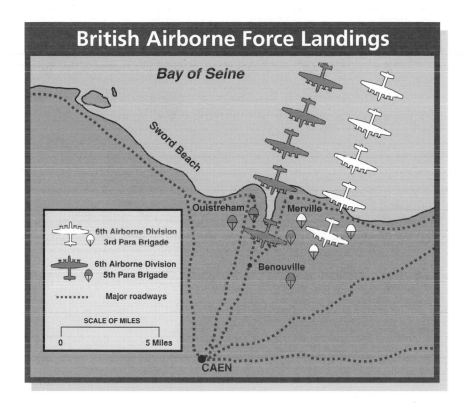

British Airborne Force Landings

Bay of Seine

Sword Beach

Ouistreham

Merville

Benouville

CAEN

6th Airborne Division
3rd Para Brigade

6th Airborne Division
5th Para Brigade

Major roadways

SCALE OF MILES

0   5 Miles

D day Bomber Command repeatedly attempted to do so. The battery's walls consisted of steel and concrete six and a half feet thick. Two of its guns were also protected by earthen banks. The battery was further defended not only by two hundred soldiers in machine-gun nests and rifle pits, but also by a treacherous minefield, barbed wire, and an electrified fence.

Just after midnight on D day, one hundred Lancaster bombers, giving airpower one last try, dropped four thousand-pound bombs on the area. Not one bomb landed on target. Part two of the plan now called for the men of Lt. Colonel Terence Otway's 9th Battalion, aided by three gliders full of reinforcements, to storm the battery at approximately 0430. They could not afford to be late, not only because the Sword landing was scheduled for 0725, but more importantly because at 0530 shelling of the area would begin from the HMS *Arethusa* stationed offshore. Anyone nearby—German or British—stood an excellent chance of being blown to bits.

Things began poorly for Otway. Of his five hundred paratroopers only 150 collected at the appointed meeting spot. Even worse, gliders scheduled to meet him with much-needed flamethrowers, mine detectors, mortars, and ladders were blown off course and never arrived.

By 0430 what there was of the 9th Battalion waited outside the battery, ready to attack. Otway's men cut the wires on the electrified fence and were about to attack when a nervous herd

British Ingenuity

Each paratrooper carried with him a variety of deadly weapons. One of their favorites was the so-called Bannon Bomb, an explosive device invented in the North African campaign of 1942. It was not devised by a team of highly-trained munitions experts or in any top-secret laboratory or arsenal. It was instead created in the field by Lieutenant Jock Bannon of the British 1st Parachute Brigade.

The Bannon Bomb was the essence of simplicity, and despite its light weight it packed a deadly punch. The Bannon Bomb consisted of two pounds of plastic explosive (with an igniting device in the middle) which was tightly packed into a black bag. The bag would then be thrown at a German tank, with the explosion capable of damaging the tank's steel outer shell and even possibly ripping off a portion of its revolving gun turret.

One disadvantage of the Bannon Bomb was its short life span. This was not because of any design flaw, but because resourceful British and American paratroopers soon discovered they could handily break off small pieces of the explosive and use them to start campfires. The result was a fighting force well supplied with piping hot coffee or tea, but with increasingly smaller Bannon Bombs at its disposal to hurl at enemy tanks.

of cows grazing outside the battery stampeded and alerted the Germans, who immediately opened fire.

If the mission were to succeed Otway had but one choice, attack no matter how high the losses. His commandos raced through the minefield. Many tripped mines and were killed, but still they moved forward and overwhelmed the enemy. The paratroopers killed 178 Germans. Only 80 men of the 9th Battalion were still in fighting condition; the rest were either dead or wounded.

Racing against the clock, Otway's remaining troops blew up the battery. By 0445 the operation was over, but Otway moved on for more action. As is so often the case in war, irony accompanied his mission. The guns he captured were only half the size intelligence had reported. And after he marched away the Germans returned and repaired two of the guns. Within two days they would be used to fire at Sword.

The German Response

On the German side the Seventh Army's Major General Max Pemsel informed Rommel's chief of staff, Major General Hans Speidel: "The air landings constitute the first phase of a larger enemy action." He added ominously that "engine noises are audible from out at sea." Speidel would not believe him. His official war diary entry read: "Chief of Staff Army Group B believes that for the time being this is not to be considered as a large operation."

At first Admiral Theodor Krancke, German naval commander in the west, agreed with Speidel. So did Speidel's superiors in Paris: "Operation OB West holds that this is not a large-scale airborne operation, all the more because Admiral Channel Coast [the headquarters of Admiral Krancke] has reported that the enemy had dropped straw dummies." The German generals had clearly been fooled by the Allies' fake paratroopers.

As more information came in, however, Krancke quickly changed his mind. He ordered his 5th E-Boat Flotilla, based at Le Havre, into action. Only three of its six vessels were ready to go, but Lieutenant Commander Heinrich Hoffmann led the three into action anyway. Hoffmann, in the first boat, beheld a huge array of British warships. "I felt I was sitting in a rowboat," he later admitted, but, nonetheless, he ordered a torpedo attack. His three patrol boats launched eighteen torpedoes toward the British fleet. One hit the boiler room of the Norwegian destroyer *Svenner*, and the ship sank rapidly. Hoffmann, not wanting to push his luck, ordered a quick retreat, but had enough presence of mind to attempt to warn the rest of Normandy's German defenders. He radioed the news of a massive invasion back to his home base of Le Havre—but the message never got there. In the action, his radio had been knocked out.

Assessing Success

Allied paratroop landings enjoyed only mixed success. Several important objectives, such as Ste.-Mere-Eglise and a few bridges and gun emplacements, were captured. Casualties were less than expected, but parachute landings were so scattered that in many cases troops could muster only a small fraction of their strength for any action. Paratroopers landed as much as seventy miles away from their planned drop zones. Never again would a night landing be attempted.

Yet such scattered landings did produce tremendous confusion among the Germans. They did not know where to respond. Landings were occurring all around them. American general Omar Bradley thought the creation of such chaos made the air landings a success despite all their failings. "Only a few units were able to organize and fight as planned," he admitted. "However, the sudden presence of 24,000 paratroopers behind the Atlantic Wall in Normandy created immense confusion and fear among the German defenders, and that alone justified their deployment."

CHAPTER FIVE

The British and Canadian Beaches

British and Canadian forces assembling for Overlord had a score to settle with the Germans. The British army had been run off the European continent at Dunkirk; the Canadians lost 3,648 of 5,100 troops at Dieppe. Both wished to avenge defeat by beating the Germans in combat in France. Now they had their chance.

Starting on June 2, thirty-eight British and Canadian convoys, led by the HMS *Scylla*, the flagship of Rear Admiral Sir Philip Vian, steamed toward Sword, Juno, and Gold Beaches. A hero of the war, Vian had distinguished himself by sinking the German battleship *Bismarck* in May 1941.

The assault troops all belonged to General Sir Miles C. Dempsey's British Second Army (the "British Liberation Army"), which despite its name also included Canadian detachments. Their landings would cover a sector twenty-five miles wide. Aside from facing Rommel's frontline units on the beaches, they also were in danger from the 21st Panzer Division based near Caen.

Topographically the British and Canadians faced an easier time of it than did the Americans. There were no high cliffs like at Omaha Beach, no flooded areas behind the German defenders as at Utah. Yet after leaving the beaches British and Canadian objectives were more difficult than the Americans': capturing the cities of Bayeux and Caen in order to secure the Allies' eastern flank.

Sword Beach

Sword Beach was the easternmost of the five landing areas. In May Rommel had visited the site and matter-of-factly predicted to his battery officers, "If they come, they will come here." The Allies expected Sword to be the most heavily defended of the three Commonwealth beaches. One British recruit was coldly informed that "all of us in the first wave would probably be wiped out." Eighty-four percent casualties were expected.

Boosting chances for survival on Sword, however, was Colonel Otway's success in destroying the Merville battery that would have rained deadly fire down upon the beach.

The first Commonwealth forces to go ashore were the men of the 22nd Dragoon Guards. Supported by five minesweeping flail tanks, they touched down on Sword Beach and were immediately hit hard.

"They were flung about as German machine-gun fire hit them," observed Corporal Charles Baldwin, "clutching various parts of their bodies, jolted like rag dolls, then sinking into the water. I often wondered if any of those unfortunate men survived the landing. Even slightly wounded, the weight of their equipment dragged them under."

The flail tanks' first task was to clear the area of mines and obstacles. The next was to turn their 75-millimeter guns on German positions. Immediately behind them were twenty landing

A body of British troops marches off to attack after having landed in their assault boats. Soldiers crouch against enemy fire as they atttempt to dig in and secure the beachhead.

The Funnies

The invaders needed mobile armored firepower on the Normandy beaches, but landing tanks in storm-tossed waters and on rocky beaches was no easy task.

The Dieppe invasion failed in part because of a deficiency of armored units, and Prime Minister Churchill wanted to avoid the same mistake. Accordingly, he ordered Major General Percy C.S. Hobart to develop tanks that could surmount virtually any landing difficulty. His new tanks would be dubbed "the Funnies," but the Germans who saw them coming straight at them on D day were not laughing.

The D.D. (Duplex Drive) tank was originally not Hobart's idea, but he had perfected it. Tanks were always at risk of sinking as they came ashore; Hobart took a thirty-three-ton Sherman tank, powered it with dual rear-mounted propellers (hence the name Duplex Drive) and surrounded it with a watertight canvas flotation collar that stretched from its treads to above its turrets. The Americans mockingly called the D.D.s "Donald Ducks," but that did not stop them from using a few of them on D day—and wishing they had more.

Another essential Hobart invention was the flail tank, a Sherman tank on the front of which a ten-foot-wide metal drum was mounted above ground level. On the drum were long, heavy metal chains. As the tank moved forward the drum rotated at high speed. The chains flew about ("flailed") and hit the ground in front of the tank, detonating any mine that lay in the sand. Neither drum nor tank would be directly hit. The British nicknamed the flail "the Crab."

Hobart's "bobbin" tank was a variation of the British-made Churchill tank. Mounted in front was a treadmill of coir, a very coarse and durable material manufactured from coconut husks. The tank would ride forward on this sturdy mat, enabling it to advance on slippery clay. When a bobbin tank had to fire on the enemy, the mechanism holding the treadmill could be lowered to the ground to make room for its gun.

Still another of Hobart's many "Funnies" transported a forty-foot box-girder bridge for crossing tank ditches and other obstacles, both natural and German-made.

The "Donald Duck," with its inflatable collar. Upon landing, the collar had to be deflated and dropped in order for the gunner to fire.

craft carrying the 1st South Lancashires and 2nd East Yorkshires. Twenty minutes later another wave of British troops landed.

Berets and Bagpipes

Lord Simon "Shimy" Lovat's 1st Special Service Brigade was among the first to land on Sword. This commando unit's mission was to reinforce the paratroopers who had earlier seized the Orne River bridges. Lovat had promised Major General Richard "Dickie" Gale, head of the 6th Airborne, that his jaunty troops (they wore green berets instead of helmets; helmets were not "manly") would link up with the paratroopers "sharp at noon."

Not only berets but taste in music set Lovat's troops apart. The commandos sloshed ashore to the screeching notes of the brigade's bagpiper, William Millin. "Give us 'Highland Laddie,'" ordered Lovat. Other tunes, like "The Road to the Isles" followed, as the men rushed past Millin shouting, "That's the stuff, Jock" [a Scottish nickname for a country boy].

Lovat found the going rougher than expected and did not meet his noon goal for reinforcing the paratroopers. But at 1330, the 6th Airborne, still busy fighting Germans, thought they heard the sound of bagpipes coming toward them. It *was* bagpipes; Millin was wailing out the old Scottish Highlands tune "Blue Bonnets over the Border" as he led the commandos up from the beach.

The troops of the 6th Airborne were not the only ones amazed by the sound. So were the Germans, who actually stopped firing for a while as the British troops hooked up. Lovat glanced down at his watch and extended apologies to his comrades for being "a couple of minutes late."

Quoting the Bard

Bagpipes were not the only unusual inspiration British commanders devised for their troops at Sword. Major C.K. "Banger" King, an assault boat commander with the East Yorkshires, rallied his men with a passage from William Shakespeare's play *Henry V*, the story of another English invasion of France, in October 1415 during the Hundred Years' War. The young British monarch's stirring address to his troops before they met the French at the decisive Battle of Agincourt is among the most famous in all literature.

Bounced by the choppy waves of the English Channel, King shouted his words into his landing craft's loudspeaker, reminding his men that in years to come their deeds would still be remembered. "And gentlemen of England now a-bed," King roared, "shall think themselves accurs'd they were not here. . . . He that outlives this day and comes safe home, Will stand a tip-toe when this day is named."

Heading Inland from Sword

The 41st Commando Brigade, despite a difficult landing, headed west toward Lion-sur-Mer, which French civilians mistakenly told them had been abandoned by the Germans. As they approached the village, however, all hell broke loose. Machine-gun and sniper fire rained down on them. The British took the village but *Wehrmacht* artillery fire destroyed three British tanks.

Meanwhile the 2nd East York Regiment, augmented by troops from the 4th and 10th Commando Brigades, headed for Ouistreham. As early as 0900 they had driven a mile and a half inland.

By 1600 the King's Shropshire Light Infantry had captured Bieville, only three miles from Caen. That city had suffered an incredibly heavy air bombardment, and refugees streamed from its ruins. Between Caen and the British, however, was the 21st Panzer Division. The Germans clearly knew they were playing for high stakes. *Wehrmacht* general Erich Marks had bluntly told tank commander Colonel Hermann von Oppeln-Bronikowski: "Oppeln, the future of Germany may very well rest on your shoulders. If you don't push the British back into the sea, we've lost the war."

But it was not only at Sword Beach that Germans faced off against Britons. Gold Beach also saw fierce fighting.

British "Tommies" land on the Normandy beaches. Britons played a key role in the invasion, especially at Gold and Sword Beaches.

Winston Churchill Reporting for Duty, Sir

Prime Minister Winston Churchill was never shy; neither was he afraid of gunfire. During the Boer War of 1899–1903, in which Britain fought the Dutch (Boer) republics of South Africa, he had been captured by the Boers and won international fame for his daring escape.

Now, nearly a half century later, the sixty-nine-year-old Churchill was still ready for action. He beseeched General Eisenhower to allow him to observe the D day invasion from the deck of the HMS *Belfast*, off the Normandy coast. Eisenhower, of course, told him it was impossible to needlessly risk one of the Allied leaders.

Churchill, not satisfied with the answer, told Ike: "You have operational command of all forces, but you are not responsible administratively for the makeup of the crews." Eisenhower thought about that, and when he agreed, Churchill shot back, "Well, then, I can sign on as a member of the crew of one of His Majesty's ships, and there's nothing you can do about it."

"That's correct," admitted Eisenhower. "But, Prime Minister, you will make my burden a lot heavier if you do it."

Churchill still insisted on his scheme. Eisenhower, realizing that a frontal assault against the stubborn prime minister was futile, tried a flanking attack. He had his chief of staff, General Walter Bedell Smith, phone King George VI to have His Majesty personally intercede. The king, father of current English monarch Queen Elizabeth II, told Smith, "You boys leave Winston to me." But even he was not about to challenge Churchill directly. He called Churchill and said, "As long as you feel that it is desirable to go along, I think it is my duty to go along with you."

Only at that point did Churchill finally abandon his reckless idea.

Gold Beach

Gold was the westernmost of the three Commonwealth beaches. To the west of Juno and ten miles east of Omaha Beach, it was assigned to the British 50th Division. That unit would be followed on the beach by the 7th Armoured Division, the "Desert Rats," which had distinguished itself in North Africa.

As at the four other beaches, at Gold a tremendous air and naval bombardment preceded the first landings. Many of the shells fell inland on the French inhabitants of the area. "The bombing was intensified and seemed to be coming nearer," wrote Mademoiselle Genget of the village of St.-Come-de-Fresne. "We had the impression that all sorts of things were falling in the courtyard. We were not feeling very brave!"

The 1st Hampshire Regiment, near the small town of Le Hamel, and the 5th East Yorkshires, near La Riviere, both met heavy artillery fire. The 47th Royal Marine Commandos sent six-

From New France to Old

The nation of Canada is an uneasy partnership of English- and French-speaking peoples. In World War I French-Canadians (concentrated mainly in the province of Quebec) had little interest in serving in the Canadian armed forces. Although French-Canadians then accounted for 20 percent of the Canadian population, they made up just 4.5 percent of its fighting forces.

In World War II that situation changed significantly, as French-Canadians made up 15 percent of the Canadian navy and fifteen of the seventy-five Canadian infantry battalions.

Manning one of the Canadian Duplex Drive tanks at Juno was French-Canadian sergeant Leo Gariepy. His vehicle rolled up the beach and was the first tank to arrive at the village of Courseulles, but a civilian truck blocked his path on one of the village's narrow streets. He spied two men and a woman standing in a nearby doorway, just staring at the Canadians. He presumed they owned the truck "so I . . . told them in good Quebec French, 'Now will you please move that truck out of the way so I can get by?'"

Still they stared. "So then," Gariepy recalled, "I called them everything I could think of in the military vocabulary. They were amazed to hear a Tommy [English soldier]—they thought we were Tommies—speak French with the old Norman dialect!"

Gariepy's tirade had its effect. The truck was moved and the tanks passed through.

teen boats in their first wave. Four sank outright and eleven more were so badly damaged they could not return to the mother ship. One of the LCAs (Landing Craft, Assault) that sank went down fifty yards away from shore. The crew's equipment went to the bottom with it. Adding to their problems was heavy machine-gun fire. "Perhaps we're intruding," one sergeant wondered aloud, "This seems to be a private beach." Other Britons also retained a sense of dark humor in the face of heavy German fire. From a rocket-firing barge off Gold a recording of the song "We Don't Know Where We're Going" blared out.

The British realized that tides were coming in faster than expected, giving their demolition teams almost no time to dismantle enough German mines and boobytraps to enable their Duplex Drive tanks to land. Yet, remembering the lesson of Dieppe—that infantrymen by themselves stood almost no chance of success—the tanks came in anyway. They helped win the day, and the fight for Gold went like clockwork as the British pushed aside relatively weak German resistance. The beach was soon in Allied hands.

The 50th Division took Le Hamel but found the going tough all the way up to La Riviere two and a half miles beyond. Once there, however, the advance became significantly easier. One German battalion collapsed completely and launched into a wild headlong retreat. Other German battalions futilely attempted to fill the breach, but the Britons plunged ahead regardless. By day's end the British were six miles inland and within one mile of the city of Bayeux.

Juno Beach

Juno, the only beach assigned to the Canadians, was situated between Gold and Sword. Thoughts of another catastrophe on the scale of Dieppe haunted the Canadians, but at Juno the odds had shifted heavily in their favor. "At Dieppe the Germans had opposed six battalions with two and a half. On Juno they were to oppose nine battalions with less than one," notes John Keegan, author of *Six Armies in Normandy: From D-Day to the Liberation of Paris.* That translated into just 400 Germans facing a Canadian first wave of 2,400 men, supported by 76 amphibious tanks and massive air and sea bombardments. But more than numbers favored the Canadians. Their troops were mature, fit, and well trained. Many of the Germans of the 716th Infantry Division were very young or very old. Many had been wounded while fighting with other units. And although earlier in the war the Germans had distinguished themselves in the art of lightning-quick mobile blitzkrieg, those days were over. The soldiers of the 716th were lucky if they had a bicycle to ride. Horses pulled their artillery.

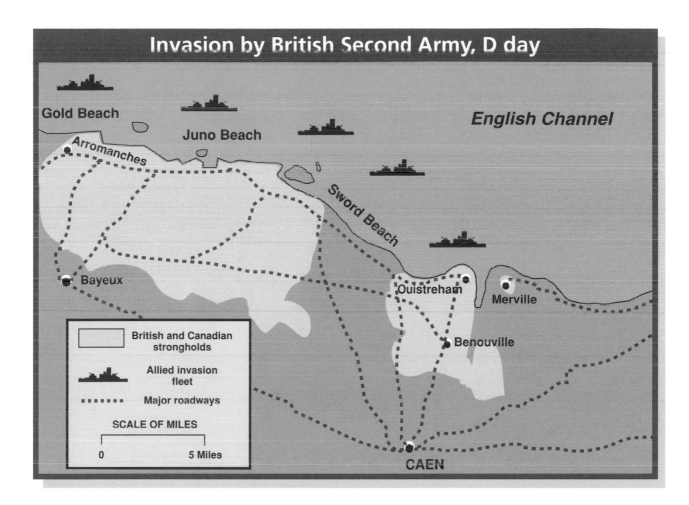

Invasion by British Second Army, D day

Gold Beach

Juno Beach

English Channel

Arromanches

Sword Beach

Bayeux

Ouistreham

Merville

Benouville

British and Canadian strongholds

Allied invasion fleet

Major roadways

SCALE OF MILES

0   5 Miles

CAEN

Beginning at 0600, first the British Bomber Command and then the U.S. Eighth Air Force blasted German positions at Juno, again with very little success; some of their bombs landed as far as three miles off target. At this point in the war, the Germans were all too accustomed to bombardment, and at first did not regard this hellish air and naval attack as anything particularly unusual. At 0645, the Seventh Army reported to von Rundstedt: "Purpose of naval bombardment not yet apparent. It appears to be a covering action in conjunction with attacks to be made at other points later."

But as the shelling continued and grew more intense, it became clear that something major was about to happen. Yet despite the fury of this attack, only about 14 percent of all concrete bunkers guarding the beaches were destroyed. Eighty percent of the German fortifications were still functioning as the Canadians came ashore. That meant the Germans could throw the firepower of mortars, machine guns, 50-millimeter, 75-millimeter, and 88-millimeter guns at the advancing Canadians. Also aiding the Germans were the 14,000 mines they had sown on the 4-mile-wide stretch of beach.

The Canadians had originally been scheduled to land at 0735, but their landing was delayed ten minutes so that the rising tide could provide their landing craft greater protection from what they believed were jagged rocks dotting the beach. In fact, what aerial reconnaissance had thought to be "rocks" were instead huge clumps of seaweed. Even this minimal delay meant that the Canadian demolition teams would have less time to clear away the German traps and obstacles and that while they were struggling with their task they would be partially underwater.

The Canadians also landed far from their intended target. Instead of landing aside the heaviest concentration of obstacles, they would have to charge right through it.

Some units, such as the Regina Rifle Regiment, the Royal Winnipeg Rifles, and the Queen's Own Rifles of Canada, suffered heavy losses. The Queen's Own Rifles lost half their men in just a few minutes. "The Germans were anywhere but with their hands down," noted a commander of one of the Canadians' assault craft. "They had made a rapid recovery from the very heavy bombardment, and were firing very actively, although the firing to start with was hesitant and spasmodic, but mortars were already ranging and machine guns were firing concentrated bursts."

One Major de Stackpoole of the British 48th Royal Marine Commandos (some British units also landed at Juno) was hit in both thighs even before his craft sank on the way to the beach.

British and Canadian troops wade onto the beach at Juno. The troops delayed the landing until the tide was higher, in order to protect landing craft from jagged rocks.

He swam towards another boat, but when he found it was heading back to England, he screamed, "Nonsense! You're all bloody well mad!" and then dived into the English Channel and headed for shore.

As in all combat, the violence was both horrific and surreal. At St.-Abuin-sur-Mer heavy German fire forced one Allied tank to scurry about in evasive action. As it careened about the beach, it ran over dead and dying Canadians. Captain Daniel Flunder of the 48th Royal Marine Commandos was incensed. He headed for the tank, beating on its hatch with his swagger stick and shouting, "They're my men!" When he got no response, Flunder pulled out a hand grenade and hurled it at the tank, blowing off one of its treads.

Helping to turn the tide for the Canadians was the arrival of their amphibious Duplex Drive Sherman tanks. Their appearance alone stunned the German defenders. "It was quite amazing," recalled one tank sergeant. "I still remember very vividly some of the machine gunners standing up in their posts looking at us with their mouths wide open. To see tanks coming out of the water shook them rigid."

Canadian soldiers—and their bicycles—await landing at Normandy.

"Monty"

Though American general Dwight Eisenhower had overall command of the Allied Expeditionary Force, command of Overlord Allied ground forces (the 21st Army Group) fell to British general Bernard Law Montgomery.

The son of an Anglican bishop, Montgomery was raised in Tasmania in Australia but graduated from Sandhurst, the British West Point, in 1908 and served as a captain in World War I, where he was twice wounded.

As World War II began he commanded a division in France and was evacuated with the rest of the British army at Dunkirk. He oversaw the controversial and unsuccessful raid at Dieppe, but quickly redeemed his reputation fighting in North Africa. Placed in command of the British Eighth Army, he stopped Rommel at El Alamein in late 1942 and in 1943 defeated him once more at the Battle of Mareth Line in Tunisia. Also in 1943 he played a key role in the invasions of Sicily and the Italian mainland.

In December 1943 Eisenhower gave Montgomery command of Overlord land operations. Throughout the war, however, Montgomery battled—both privately and publicly—with Eisenhower. Many observers described him as egotistical, but others—as well as Montgomery himself—praised Montgomery as the finest British field commander since the Duke of Wellington in the Napoleonic Wars.

Prime Minister Churchill promoted "Monty" to field marshal in August 1944. In 1946, in honor of his North African victories, King George VI named him 1st Viscount of Alamein. From 1951 to 1958 Montgomery served as deputy commander of the NATO (North Atlantic Treaty Organization) military alliance.

Bernard Montgomery was a controversial figure in much the same way as U.S. general Douglas MacArthur. He often disagreed—publicly—with his commanding officer, and also, like MacArthur, had a very high opinion of himself.

Despite the rough going several units experienced, the Canadians still suffered far fewer casualties than had been projected. It was thought they might lose 2,000 men, including 600 by drowning. But by day's end, they had suffered a total of just 1,000 casualties, including 335 dead.

Not only had the Canadians avoided another Dieppe, but as D day ended one advance party composed of the North Nova Scotia Highlanders and the Sherbrooke Fusiliers had driven ten miles toward the Bayeux-Caen highway and the Carpiquet airport. They were farther inland than any other landing force.

CHAPTER SIX

The American Beaches

Twenty-one convoys sat offshore from the American beaches of Omaha and Utah in the darkness before D day. At 0345 on the morning of June 6, twelve miles off the Normandy coast, Americans began boarding their small assault craft. They would spend hours aboard these small, wave-tossed craft before storming ashore.

When they reached land they would find circumstances vastly different from one beach to the other: an almost textbook, i.e., flawless, assault on Utah and a near disaster at Omaha, soon to be known as "Bloody Omaha."

Iles-St.-Marcouf

The first American amphibious landing, however, did not occur at either Omaha or Utah, but on the tiny Iles-St.-Marcouf, three miles off Utah. These two small, rocky islands had not been part of Overlord planning until mid-May. Prior to that, the Allies—despite excellent reconnaissance—had not even known of their existence. However, once Allied strategists learned of them, concern grew. Could these islands contain deadly German gun emplacements, putting Utah's landing forces at risk of fire from their rear?

This possibility could not be ignored. At 0430, 132 men from the U.S. 4th and 24th Cavalries stormed ashore on the islands. They discovered neither artillery nor Germans. Instead they found only deadly "S" mines. Two Americans died and 17 others were wounded to capture this virtually worthless objective.

Utah Beach

Utah Beach was the beach closest to Ste.-Mere-Eglise, and that was a great advantage to 4th Infantry Division troops that would wade ashore there at sunrise. Most of their work had already been done by the 82nd and 101st Airborne Divisions. The paratroopers had not only provided a diversion but had seized a fair portion of the territory to the rear of the Germans at Utah. Ste.-Mere-Eglise was already in American hands. General James Gavin held positions at Merderet and Douve. General Maxwell Taylor's 101st Airborne had captured the Germans' gun battery at St.-Martin-de-Varreville.

(Below) U.S. soldiers disembark from a landing barge to dash through the surf and up the beach under fire from Nazi defenders. Such barges scurried back and forth to continually bring reinforcements (right) to the beaches of Normandy.

At Utah, only a few German artillery shells were launched at the American invaders, doing little more damage than showering the assault boats with relatively harmless fragments. Although one barge loaded with four amphibious tanks hit a mine when it dropped its ramp, twenty-eight of the Americans' thirty-two tanks successfully reached land and began blazing away at the *Wehrmacht* almost instantly. Within an hour the entire beach was cleared. "The landing just wasn't a big deal at all," admitted one GI.

That was not entirely true. Far more damaging than German firepower at Utah was the savage force of the English Channel. To begin with, it mercilessly rocked the LCTs (Landing Craft, Tanks) and LCAs (Landing Craft, Assault) that were heading toward shore. The men aboard were helplessly seasick. Seven of the LCTs sank outright.

The current swept the Americans far from where they should have landed. Heavy smoke from the naval bombardment preceding the attack obscured the shore. It was not until the Americans landed that they learned they were more than a mile south of their intended destination.

Soldiers carrying supplies disembark onto the beaches at Normandy. Sheer luck would determine whether these soldiers would face murderous heavy fire or relatively little.

Yet even that mistake boded well for the Americans. Originally they were scheduled to land at Utah Beach's most heavily defended section. Instead they came ashore at the beach's least fortified area. And just beyond where they landed, the 82nd and 101st Airborne Divisions stood a short distance away.

"Start the War from Here"

Ashore at Utah Beach was Brigadier General Theodore Roosevelt Jr., the son of President Theodore Roosevelt and the cousin of President Franklin D. Roosevelt.

Roosevelt was not merely the only general to land with Overlord's first wave of troops; he was also the oldest man ashore. Fifty-seven years old, he suffered from a weak heart and arthritis in his shoulders, and walked with a cane. Yet he insisted on landing with his men. "It will steady the boys to know I am with them," he offered. Roosevelt limped about the beach, oblivious to enemy fire, waving a walking stick and a pistol. He urged his GIs onward, even while comforting the wounded.

Roosevelt had to decide what to do about landing in the wrong place. Thirty thousand more men and 3,500 additional vehicles were scheduled to land upon the heels of the first wave. A choice had to be made—and soon. Chaos and thousands of deaths could result if Roosevelt's choice was wrong.

Roosevelt thought a moment, then decided he would march inland from where he stood, telling his officers: "We're going to start the war from here."

Beyond Utah

In landing 23,000 men at Utah, the 4th Division had suffered just 197 dead or wounded, plus another 60 missing and presumed drowned. Yet Utah Beach was not entirely a success story. While the Americans had gotten off to a good, indeed miraculous, start, they soon bogged down and fell well behind their established timetable.

First they were distracted when some units *did* march north to capture their original objectives. Resistance from the German 709th Division continued to be light, but the Americans still lost valuable time.

More significant delays occurred as the troops marched inland, heading into a virtually impassable swamp. Burdened with sixty-eight pounds of gear, they sank deep into the muck—and even further behind schedule.

Allied soldiers faced almost unbelievable odds on the beaches of Normandy. Not only were they attacked by Nazi soldiers training their guns on them from land, the heavy sea of the English Channel made the men seasick before they disembarked. Here men are helped after their landing craft was sunk by the Germans.

"The Man Who Won the War"

Dwight Eisenhower commanded a huge army in England. Getting that army to France was the problem. To solve it the soldiers of the Normandy invasion, as well as those in North Africa and the Pacific, disembarked from their destroyers and cruisers onto LCAs (Landing Craft, Assault).

The LCAs, or "Higgins boats," were invented and manufactured by Andrew Jackson Higgins of New Orleans. Eisenhower was so impressed by their success in getting men ashore that twenty years later he praised Higgins as "the man who won the war for us."

Andrew Higgins was an unlikely war hero. Before Pearl Harbor his company had not amounted to much. He drank heavily and had a ferocious temper, but when it came to designing small boats he had few equals. The cigar-box-shaped LCAs were 36 feet long and 10 ½ feet wide. Their sides were made of plywood. A metal ramp in the front brought a full platoon of 36 men to the shoreline, then the craft would quickly return for another load.

Higgins eventually employed 30,000 workers to manufacture 20,094 Higgins boats and PT boats. Over his factory floor hung a sign proclaiming "The Man Who Relaxes Is Helping the Axis."

However, the men who actually rode Higgins boats on D day were not as impressed as Eisenhower. They were tossed about by giant waves and more often than not were violently seasick. One 4th Division GI, weak and sick, spoke for many. "That guy Higgins," he moaned, "ain't got nothin' to be proud of inventin' this goddamned boat."

Omaha Beach: Valuable Real Estate

Utah Beach was 20 miles from Gold Beach, the westernmost British beach. Steep, virtually impenetrable cliffs guarded the intervening stretch of coastline. Only at Omaha was there a beach even remotely suitable for a landing. Even then the beach was only 300 feet deep. Beyond the beach were 100-foot-high cliffs, heavily guarded by Germans in pillboxes and bunkers using mortars, multibarreled rocket launchers, and machine guns. Leading south from those fortifications were just 4 thoroughfares, only one of which was a paved road. The others were mere cart paths. Beyond that were the villages of Vierville, Saint-Laurent-sur-Mer, and Colleville-sur-Mer, which the Germans had heavily fortified. And beyond that was the Aure Valley, which the *Wehrmacht* had flooded to further impede any invasion's progress.

About the only thing the Americans had in their favor at Omaha Beach was that while it was heavily fortified, those fortifications were not heavily manned. Allied reconnaissance in the planning stages revealed that only 800 to 1,000 *Wehrmacht* troops held Omaha. And about half were not even Germans; they were Poles and Russians who had been forced into the *Wehrmacht* and had little stake in a German victory. At the first opportunity most would be only too happy to surrender to the Allies. Against these ill-trained, apathetic men on the first morning of the assault the Americans would throw a first wave of 34,000 well-armed, well-trained, highly motivated soldiers.

Just one week before D day, however, the situation changed radically. The *Wehrmacht*'s battle-hardened 352nd Infantry Division moved up from St. Lo to engage in antilanding maneuvers. Now, facing a larger and tougher enemy, Allied chances at Omaha were slim.

The Allies' Strategy at Omaha

Because of the difficult terrain and the strong German defenses, Omaha was the only beach to which two divisions were assigned. After the first assault wave a follow-up force of 34,000 troops and 3,300 vehicles would land throughout the morning. At noon (1200) a third wave of 25,000 GIs and 4,400 vehicles would begin coming ashore. If the first wave faltered, a massive, and deadly, traffic jam would result on Omaha Beach, with German fire mowing down troops like sitting ducks. If the second wave did not land, other problems would arise. First, that would almost guarantee that Omaha would not be taken. Secondly, if troops originally destined for Omaha Beach were shifted to any of the four other beaches, the resulting congestion might jeopardize success there.

Omaha's landing plan divided the beach into seven sectors: Dog Green, Dog White, Dog Red, Easy Green, Easy Red, Fox Green, and Fox Red. Major General Charles H. Gerhardt's 116th Infantry Regiment would attack on the western sector of Omaha, between Vierville and Saint-Laurent-sur-Mer, i.e., Dog Green, Dog White, Dog Red, and Easy Green. Major General Clarence R. Huebner's 18th Infantry Regiment would land on the east, between Saint-Laurent-sur-Mer and Colleville-sur-Mer, i.e., Easy Red, Fox Green, and Fox Red. All of these troops had seen difficult combat in North Africa and Sicily and had rehearsed over and over again what they would find and what they would do on Omaha.

That was the first wave. Following these regiments, other portions of the U.S. V Corps 1st and 29th Divisions would wade ashore. The 29th Division would advance along the coast as far as the Vire estuary to the west. The 1st Division would drive east toward the British beaches and link up with the British Second Army at Port en Bessin. By nightfall on D day it was hoped a bridgehead sixteen miles wide and six miles deep would be established at Omaha Beach.

Supported by air and naval gunfire, a massive number of troops, weapons, and equipment land on the beaches of Normandy during the initial assault.

Twelve Miles Out

The Allied leadership, however, committed several tactical errors that made their task much more difficult. British admiral Sir Bertram Ramsey advised Rear Admiral Alan G. Kirk, who commanded the American naval task force, to bring his ships to within eight miles of the shore. Kirk, though, feared being hit by German land batteries and instead kept his ships eleven to twelve miles offshore. At that distance from the coast, waves and winds were far worse and problems of seasickness were aggravated.

At 0345 the 16th Division's 2nd and 3rd Battalions debarked from the USS *Henrico* and the HMS *Empire Anvil*. They were scheduled to land at 0630. The Americans landed on time, but that was about all that went right on Omaha.

An official U.S. military history summarizes how poorly things went:

Heavy seas, numerous underwater obstacles and intense enemy fire destroyed many craft and caused high casualties before the assault battalions reached shore. Most supporting weapons, including D.D. tanks, were swamped. The 2nd Battalion landed between 100 to 1,000 yards from its scheduled points and was pinned down on the beach by extremely heavy fire from concrete fortifications, machine-gun emplacements and sniper nests which remained intact through severe naval and air bombardment.

As at Utah, heavy cloud cover thwarted the bombing over Omaha. Unsure of their position, and not wanting to pummel their own men, Eighth Air Force bombers erred on the side of caution. They waited just a few seconds longer before dropping their payloads, and most often missed the Germans entirely. Bombs fell harmlessly in the fields behind the *Wehrmacht* defenses, which remained unharmed and ready for action.

As a heavy naval bombardment progressed, thousands of American GIs were heading toward shore. Their thoughts had shifted from the battle they were about to face to the horrible seasickness they were suffering, as the violent waves of the English Channel tossed their craft about like toy boats sloshing about in a giant bathtub. It was not uncommon for soldiers, sick to their stomachs from hours of buffeting, to be covered with their own vomit.

Ships move toward the Normandy beaches. Fraught with danger, soldiers first had to hope that their landing craft would not be capsized by the rough surf. Upon landing and wading in, soldiers faced murderous Nazi fire.

Rudder's Rangers

Allied intelligence concluded that at Pointe du Hoe, overlooking the area between Omaha and Utah Beaches, the Germans had placed six 155-millimeter guns in concrete-protected positions. These guns could decimate units landing on Omaha Beach's western half.

Pointe du Hoe stood atop steep 117-foot cliffs. Scaling those cliffs and overwhelming the Germans would not be an easy task. "It can't be done," said one American officer. "Three old women with brooms could keep the Rangers from climbing the cliff."

Nonetheless, General Omar Bradley assigned Lt. Colonel James E. Rudder's Ranger Battalion to scale those cliffs and destroy the guns. From the beginning misfortune dogged Rudder. His lead boat headed for the wrong landing point, and before the error was corrected precious time was lost. Later the Germans saw his LCAs and DUKWs (amphibious trucks), coming across the water and let loose with heavy fire.

Colonel Rudder pushed forward. His men fired rockets carrying grapnels and rope ladders into the face of the cliff. They also used some DUKWs, outfitted with ladders borrowed from London firemen. The Germans resisted, firing at the Rangers and lobbing hand grenades down at them. To quiet them, the destroyer USS *Saterlee* opened fire.

Once atop the cliff, the Rangers saw the effects of the bombardment the enemy had endured. The area was almost entirely pitted by bomb craters. Not one German remained, but something else was also missing. Rudder's men looked for 155-millimeter guns, but they were not in place. The French resistance had attempted to alert the Allies that the guns had been moved but were unable to get through. The Rangers' losses seemed to have been in vain.

One mile inland, in a quiet apple orchard, Rudder's men found a deserted five-gun German battery. It appeared ready for action, but there was no evidence the Germans had ever manned the position. The Rangers placed grenades in the breeches (the portion of the gun that holds the shell) of the guns and blew them up.

The fighting was brutal. By day's end only 90 of the original 225 Rangers were still able to bear arms.

On reaching shore, events unfolded in no better fashion. Ten American LCTs, with more than three hundred soldiers aboard, were almost immediately capsized by the huge waves. Many died in the surf. Whitecaps nearly swamped many other boats. GIs battled furiously to bail out their rapidly sinking craft, often using their helmets to do so. Many artillery pieces sank, which meant that the Americans would be at a serious disadvantage on the beach.

American troops were not only seriously weakened by weather conditions; by the time they landed, they suffered from tactical errors committed by their leaders, who, unlike British and Canadian generals, were not so painfully aware of what had gone wrong at Dieppe. Accordingly, some commanders sent their men to frontally attack fortified positions without sufficient armored support.

The Commonwealth forces had landed with heavy support from Hobart's flails, bobbins, and vehicles that could spurt deadly flame at the enemy, but only a handful of D.D. tanks assisted the first wave of GIs. It would be up to American infantrymen to overcome the heavily protected Germans, and they would suffer heavy casualties in the process.

But these infantrymen could not even count on receiving the modest support that was planned. Nearly 4 miles from Easy Red, 29 D.D. tanks rumbled out from their LCTs to land. The waves, however, were too heavy for these tanks, which were made to travel only in relatively calm water. Twenty-one sank outright; 1 was hit by a landing craft and capsized. German guns destroyed 2 more. Only 5 actually made it to shore.

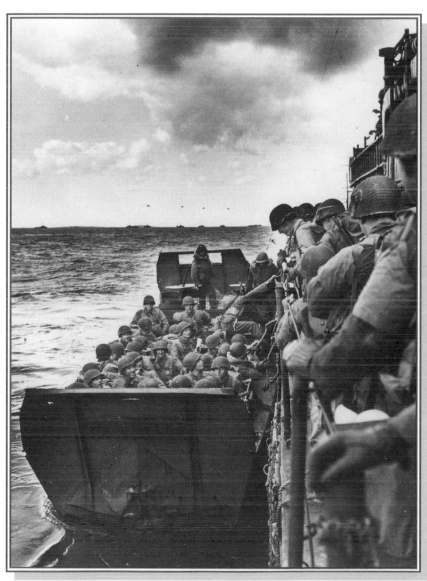

Troops are placed in a landing barge on their way toward the beaches of Normandy.

Tough Customers

Hitler had inspired a fanatic loyalty among his Nazi followers and this spilled over into the *Wehrmacht*, particularly among some of the younger officers. This was all too evident on D day. Hitler's orders were to never retreat or surrender, and some officers were determined to obey at all costs. "I saw a German officer shoot one of his men when he started to walk over to us with his hands up," recalled one American Ranger.

On D day Lance Corporal Josef Hafer of the *Wehrmacht's* 716th Division found himself trapped in a bunker, with British troops closing in. Soon the British were bringing in a flamethrower and the Germans inside were suffocating in the intense heat. An excruciating death seemed certain. Still the *Wehrmacht* captain in charge refused to surrender, even though his men begged him to do so. "It's out of the question!" he shot back. "We're going to fight our way out! Count the men and their weapons!"

Instead his men began dismantling their weapons. They would not fight. Still he refused to give up. Brandishing his machine gun, he barred his men from the door.

Finally, with the heat continuing to rise, he ordered his radio operator to reach his superior. Only when there was no response did he regain some sense of reality. "Open the door," he said spiritlessly, and allowed his men to surrender—and survive.

Meanwhile, over on Omaha's western half, there was no attempt to launch tanks in such treacherous waters. The officers in charge kept them on the LCTs. Without any way to exit the LCTs, the tanks remained onboard and the infantry were left without vital armored support.

On the Beach

The ineffective Allied air attack had been followed by an equally ferocious naval bombardment. "Look what they're doing to the Germans," said one soldier. "I guess there won't be a man alive there."

The *Wehrmacht* not only survived, however, but was ready to fire as soon as the Americans came within range, quickly pinning them down. The case of the 116th Infantry's A Company is typical. One of their six LCAs sank a half mile from shore. Another was hit by several German shells and exploded. The remaining four barely made it to land, and when their ramps lowered, the GIs did not wade ashore. Loaded down with heavy gear they jumped into churning water six feet deep.

Allied invasion troops come ashore on the beaches of Normandy. In spite of their massive numbers, Allied troops had to walk directly in the face of Nazi defenders, whose guns were trained on the soldiers, waiting to pick them off as they landed ashore.

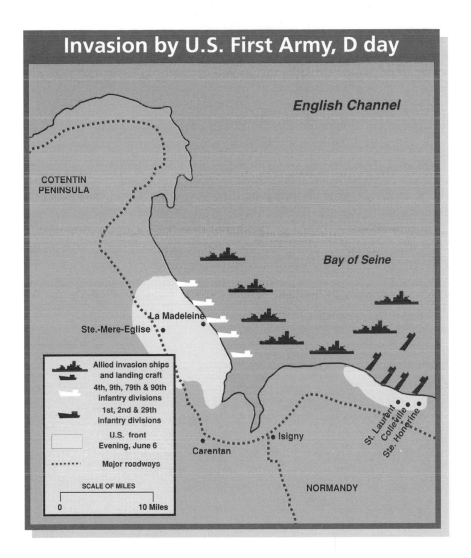

Invasion by U.S. First Army, D day

English Channel

COTENTIN
PENINSULA

Bay of Seine

La Madeleine

Ste.-Mere-Eglise

St. Laurent
Colleville
Ste. Honorine

Isigny

Carentan

NORMANDY

Allied invasion ships
and landing craft

4th, 9th, 79th & 90th
infantry divisions

1st, 2nd & 29th
infantry divisions

U.S. front
Evening, June 6

Major roadways

SCALE OF MILES

0   10 Miles

Within a few minutes, every officer and sergeant in the company had been either killed or wounded. Two-thirds of the men were casualties. The unit's official report summed up the disaster: "Within 20 minutes of striking the beach A Company had ceased to be an assault company and had become a forlorn little rescue party bent upon survival and the saving of lives."

On Omaha Beach's eastern end, things were no better. The 16th Infantry's E Company lost 105 of its 192 men. In F Company only 2 officers survived the first few minutes of fire. On one boat only 7 of 32 men managed to scramble across the beach.

The Germans saw the damage they were inflicting upon Omaha's invaders and thought they had succeeded in stopping that phase of Overlord. "The American invasion is stopped on the beaches," the German commander at Omaha gleefully radioed to his superiors. "Heavy losses are being inflicted on the survivors. The beaches are littered with burning vehicles and dead and dying troops. Heil Hitler!"

"The Dead and Those Who Are Going to Die"

Along the stretches of Omaha code-named Dog Green and Dog White, Germans pinned down the 29th Division, making it impossible for it to move up the beach.

At times like these personal heroism counted for a great deal. "It was individuals, not divisions, who determined the outcome of the day," writes author Max Hastings in *Overlord: D-Day, June 6, 1944.* Brigadier General Norman D. Cota, the 29th Division's assistant commander and the highest-ranking officer on his stretch of beach, was among the most valiant.

The fifty-one-year-old Cota thought *someone* had to rally his men. Afraid for their lives, they had been trapped on the beach for nearly two hours, going nowhere and dying one by one. Waving

Unfortunately, the Normandy invasion could not have been accomplished without the thousands of men who lost their lives on the beaches that fateful day. These men were shot and wounded, their only consolation that the Nazis could not kill all of them—some men had to get through to secure the beaches.

his .45 he strode from one end of his sector to the other, screaming over the noise of the shelling. At one point he came upon a unit and inquired who they were. "Rangers," came the response. "Then, goddammit," he stormed, "if you're Rangers get up and lead the way!" The men began creeping through barbed wire and the area's burning underbrush. Before long they were atop the bluffs, and behind the German positions.

By 1100 Cota's 29th Division had seized Vierville. But, still trapped by German obstacles, not all the Americans had left the beaches. Cota scampered back down. Spying an abandoned bulldozer loaded with TNT, he goaded a young soldier into driving it toward a group of engineers who badly needed the explosives to blast the remaining barbed wire and tank traps.

Cota commanded the right half of the 29th's sector. Colonel Charles D. Canham controlled the left. Wounded in the wrist, Canham tied a handkerchief around it and kept on rallying his men. "They're murdering us here!" he shouted. "Let's move in-

American soldiers wounded at Omaha Beach. The Germans' heavy fire destroyed whole companies of men at a time.

land and get murdered!" At first his men thought he was crazy, but they began to follow him up the beach and over the bluffs.

Similar problems arose over in the 1st Division's sector, where heavy German fire kept Americans pinned down. Like Cota and Canham, Colonel Charles A. Taylor risked his own life in an effort to get his men off the beach. "Two kinds of people are staying on this beach," he screamed, "the dead and those who are going to die. Now let's get the hell out of here!"

Withdrawal or Victory

Until officers like Cota, Canham, and Taylor rallied their men, the situation at Omaha was so precarious that General Omar Bradley seriously considered abandoning the beach and sending the scheduled follow-up waves of troops over to other beaches. The resulting confusion at those landing sites might have caused disaster there as well.

Bradley admitted, "I later remarked to Monty [General Montgomery], 'Someday I'll tell General Eisenhower just how close it was those first few hours.' I agonized over the withdrawal decision, praying that our men could hang on."

By 1330 the situation was firmly in control, and Bradley received word that "troops formerly pinned down are now advancing up heights behind the beaches."

There would be no Dieppe at Normandy.

CHAPTER SEVEN

From Normandy to Berlin

The Germans had reacted very slowly to Allied actions. Despite warnings from their frontline officers, the leadership of von Rundstedt's OB West, Rommel's Army Group B, and the German OKW all failed to respond as they should in moving troops forward to counter the invasion.

As early as 0500 Major General Max Pemsel of the *Wehrmacht's* Seventh Army warned Rommel's headquarters that a "large scale attack on Normandy is imminent."

But Army Group B waited a full hour and a half to call Rommel at his home in Herrlingen. They told him nothing about Pemsel's warning, instead informing him only of the earlier paratroop landings. Rommel, still confident that foul weather made an invasion impossible, thought this could not possibly be the real thing.

Meanwhile, phone calls were crisscrossing Europe, but no one could decide what to do. Outside Paris, Field Marshal von Rundstedt concluded, "If this is actually a large-scale enemy operation it can only be met successfully if immediate action is taken." He ordered the 12th SS

German panzer units were unable to help their comrades on the beaches of Normandy nor to respond to invading paratroopers because of bureaucratic disagreements.

(Hitler Youth) Panzer Division and the Panzer Lehr Division to head for the Atlantic coast. But these were Waffen SS (Armed SS) Divisions, not under his actual command. He needed permission for them to move and so contacted OKW, requesting it.

Von Rundstedt expected consent to be granted as a matter of course. But nothing happened. OKW chief of operations Colonel General Alfred Jodl was still asleep, and his aides were afraid to wake him. Nonetheless, one unknown member of the OKW staff phoned Hitler's Alpine retreat at Berchtesgaden. He managed to reach Hitler's naval aide, Admiral Karl von Puttkamer, who, fearing such news would set Hitler off on some irrational course of action, decided not to disturb him. Von Puttkamer simply went back to sleep. Von Rundstedt, his contempt of Hitler getting the better of him, stubbornly refused to pursue the matter.

At 1015 Rommel's headquarters called him again, this time to tell him of landings on the five beaches. Rommel now knew this was the invasion he had long feared. "How stupid of me. How stupid of me," he said in hushed tones as he hung up the phone. He canceled his planned meeting with Hitler at Berchtesgaden, summoned his car, and sped back to France.

Hitler, who kept very late hours, normally did not awake until 1000, and General Jodl, like Admiral Puttkamer, was afraid to wake him with news from Normandy. Not that it would have mattered. Once informed of events, Hitler theorized that Normandy was merely a feint and that the real invasion would still come in the Pas de Calais region. Although all 1,600 German tanks in northwestern France had been authorized by local commanders to fuel up and advance, Hitler still held them in reserve.

He was so complacent that he did not even hold his normal midday strategy session with his generals. Instead Hitler lunched with the new premier of Hungary, although he did promise aides that he would think about the matter while he ate. After lunch the Führer made his decision: the 12th SS and the Panzer Lehr Divisions could move up toward Normandy. By the time they actually received orders to do so, it was 1600, and the landings had already succeeded.

During the morning, cloud cover over France was intense. The German tanks could have moved forward relatively free from air attack. When they finally advanced they would be sitting ducks for Allied fighter planes.

The Counterattack Fails

The only German tanks to see action on D day belonged to General Edger Feuchtinger's 21st Panzer Division, which had been stationed near Caen. Feuchtinger did not wait for any orders and attacked the troops of the British 6th Airborne Division at 0630. A few hours later he received orders to disengage from attacking

Panzer divisions that did move ahead to help prevent an Allied victory at Normandy arrived after U.S. troops had managed to dig in with antitank guns and artillery. Many panzer units were destroyed by American guns.

these paratroopers and to help defend Caen. In the afternoon he attempted to split the link between Juno and Sword Beaches. Instead, Feuchtinger's tanks were greeted by heavy antitank gunfire. Then, as the day came to an end, 250 gliders full of British commandos landed to reinforce those already on the ground. It was the largest glider force to land during D day and doubled the size of the British force holding positions away from the beaches. The 21st Panzer Division, which by nightfall had lost nearly half of its 127 medium tanks, would advance no farther.

Lacking air cover, the two panzer divisions Hitler had ordered into battle also ran into trouble. Moving up to the front from Chartres, despite heavy camouflage, the Panzer Lehr Division was hit hard by Allied air attacks. By the end of June 7, the division had lost 5 tanks, 130 trucks, and 84 other armored vehicles such as self-propelled guns and half-tracks. "These losses were serious for a division not yet in action," said Panzer Lehr commander Lt. General Fritz Bayerlein, with some understatement. That was not the worst of it for Bayerlein. The next day his own staff car would be strafed; he would be wounded and his driver killed. Bayerlein's aide-de-camp would survive only by diving from the burning car into a concrete culvert.

Stalemate

By D day plus 11 (11 days after the landings) the Allies had landed 587,653 men and 89,728 vehicles in Normandy. On June 8 British tanks captured Bayeux, the first major town to be liberated.

An endless line of troop reinforcements and supply trucks headed for the front lines on the beachhead. Note the knocked out German pillbox (right).

One last German machine-gun emplacement held out at the southern end of town. The British fired into the house in which it was holed up, setting it afire. War or not, this brought out the Bayeux fire brigade. In full uniform, they ordered a halt to the firing, stormed into the house, put out the fire, and for good measure convinced the Germans to surrender.

Still the Allies were unable to make any quick breakout from the peninsula despite the fact that the Germans were virtually paralyzed in terms of troop movements. Hard-pressed everywhere, the Germans were unable to move any troops into France as they continued to be hampered by a lack of air cover. Soon they were moving only at night; they were so afraid of air strikes that to avoid detection they erased all tank tracks behind them. French resistance forces constantly sabotaged roads, bridges, railroads, and communications links. In June alone sections of the main rail line between Toulouse and Paris were blown up eight hundred times. Just as serious a liability, until late July the Germans still believed that Patton's phantom First U.S. Army Group (FUSAG) would attack in the Pas de Calais and wasted the Fifteenth Army by keeping it in reserve there.

Nonetheless, with all these disadvantages the *Wehrmacht* still bottled up the Allies in Normandy for seven weeks. Adding to the Allies' difficulties was the fact that the port of Cherbourg, which they had counted on to speed their unloading of men and supplies, was heavily damaged in the fighting. It was not fully able to receive supplies until July 19.

Caen and St.-Lo

The first major British objective in Normandy was Caen. For weeks the Germans battled fiercely and held on to the city. A new British push began on July 7, preceded by an air attack by 450 British Lancaster and Halifax bombers. After brutal house-to-house fighting the city fell on July 9.

The Germans remained firmly entrenched outside of Caen, however. Operation Goodwood attempted to drive them out, beginning on July 18. Forty-five hundred bombers dropped 7,000 tons of bombs on the Germans. Allied artillery lobbed 150,000 shells at them. Still, after losing 6,000 men and nearly 400 tanks General Montgomery's forces had advanced only 7 miles in 2 days. "It had taken 7,000 tons of bombs to gain seven miles," Eisenhower noted bitterly, "and . . . the Allies could hardly hope to go through France paying a price of 1,000 tons of bombs per mile." Air Marshall Tedder even suggested that Eisenhower fire Montgomery.

Cherbourg's harbor after Allied repairs. The harbor was heavily damaged in the fighting.

The Attack on Caen

The city of Caen was a primary strategic target of the Commonwealth forces. But the city remained out of their grasp until early July 1944 as they slowly battled through Normandy's fields and orchards. Casualties mounted. Incinerators burned through the night disposing of the uniforms of dead soldiers. Whole platoons worked full-time making white crosses for the ever-growing military cemeteries.

General Bernard Montgomery determined to avoid further losses within Caen itself. To this end he launched a massive bombing campaign, similar to that which the Americans had used against Cherbourg. There the blasting was so intense that German prisoners could not be interrogated for 24 hours—the captured Germans were temporarily deaf from the force of the bombardment.

On the night of July 7 450 bombers struck at Caen. The Allied air attack leveled the once proud medieval city. The Allies soon had cause, however, to regret their action. While the city itself had been nearly destroyed and many French were casualties, few Germans had been killed or wounded in the assault as once again Allied bombers missed their primary targets. Caen's streets were reduced to huge piles of rubble, making nearly impossible passage by Allied tanks and armored vehicles. The *Wehrmacht* dug into the debris and skillfully fought back. They blew up every bridge in the city that spanned the Orne River. Fighting was block by block and house by house. Some infantry battalions of the British Second Army took 25 percent casualties during the first 48 hours in Caen. By July 10 British and Canadian forces had gained control of Caen but at a fearsome cost both to the city, its French inhabitants, and themselves.

British soldiers take positions against a wrecked building as others go off in search of snipers lurking beyond the crumbling walls in Caen.

On July 17 Rommel was returning to his headquarters at La Roche–Guyon when two British Spitfire fighter planes strafed his automobile. They did not hit it, but Rommel's chauffeur swerved off the road and into a tree. Rommel suffered severe head injuries, which would force him out of active command of German troops.

The city of St.-Lo stood on the main road that would carry American forces west of the landings. To help defend Caen two panzer divisions had been shifted from St.-Lo to that city. St.-Lo surrendered on July 18, and the Allied tide was by now virtually irreversible. They now had 36 divisions, nearly 1.5 million troops, in Normandy. They had also landed the remarkable totals of 300,000 vehicles and about a ton of supplies per soldier. Facing these 36 Allied divisions were just 9 German divisions. On July 25 the Allied breakout from Normandy finally began.

Caen was almost completely destroyed by Allied air strikes, but, unfortunately, many Germans survived the attacks to fight the Allies (shown here), sometimes house to house, in fierce combat.

Advancing Through France

General George Patton was now commanding the new U.S. Third Army. Beginning on July 25 he raced out of the Normandy peninsula and, turning the German's flank, captured Avranches on July 31. Four days later he had cut off the Breton peninsula.

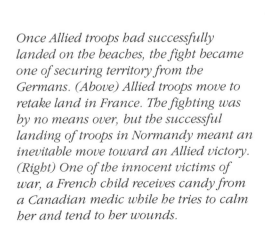

Once Allied troops had successfully landed on the beaches, the fight became one of securing territory from the Germans. (Above) Allied troops move to retake land in France. The fighting was by no means over, but the successful landing of troops in Normandy meant an inevitable move toward an Allied victory. (Right) One of the innocent victims of war, a French child receives candy from a Canadian medic while he tries to calm her and tend to her wounds.

Patton's XV Corps swung east and captured Le Mans on August 9. At the same time the Canadian First Army moved south to Falaise. This double enveloping movement caught the German 5th Panzer Division and the Seventh Army in a trap. As the Germans attempted to retreat through the one narrow avenue open to them they were mercilessly pounded by Allied planes, flying two thousand to three thousand sorties a day. It was wholesale slaughter. On August 22 this so-called Falaise Gap was closed. The Germans lost 500,000 men and their Seventh Army was destroyed as an operating entity.

General Eisenhower was saddened and sickened by what he saw after the battle was over. "I was conducted through it on foot, to encounter scenes that could only be described by Dante," he solemnly wrote. "It was literally possible to walk for hundreds of yards at a time stepping on nothing but dead and decaying flesh."

George Patton now moved to outflank Paris. On August 25 the 2nd Free French Armored Division entered the city. Parisians responded with unrestrained joy, as four years of Nazi occupation ended.

A Frenchwoman welcomes American soldiers on D day. French liberation was at hand.

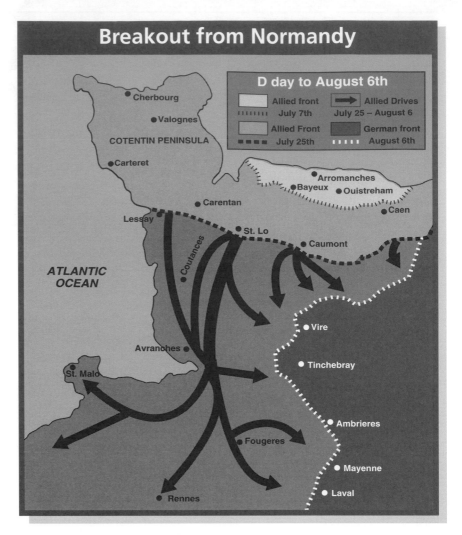

Wonder Weapons

Despite all these losses, the Nazis still maintained a victorious posture because of Hitler's so-called wonder weapons. These included such new technologies as rockets (the V-1 and V-2), the jet engine, and even the possibility of an atomic bomb. On June 6 Hitler had ordered V-1 attacks on London (code-named Junkroom). The attacks did not actually start until June 12 and would have little effect on the course of the war, but would make the Allies increasingly nervous about what other tricks Nazi science had up its sleeve.

On June 17 Hitler met with von Rundstedt and Rommel at a bunker near Soissons in northeast France. Rommel "with merciless frankness" told Hitler the war was virtually lost. Hitler shot back, "Don't you worry about the future course of the war. Look to your own invasion front" and informed Rommel that the V-1 attacks "would make the British willing to make peace."

As the meeting concluded, a V-1 aimed at London exploded atop the German bunker. No one was hurt, but it was an unmistakably negative omen.

Old Blood and Guts

General George S. "Old Blood and Guts" Patton waited patiently in England during preparations for Operation Overlord, serving to deceive German intelligence with his phantom First U.S. Army Group.

But a soldier of Patton's talents could not be kept inactive for long. Shortly after the Allies consolidated their foothold in Normandy, Eisenhower gave him command of the new U.S. Third Army. In less than ten months Patton's tank columns swept across northern France, Belgium, Luxembourg, Germany, Austria, and even into Czechoslovakia, capturing 1.5 million Germans in the process. "We shall attack and attack," boasted Patton, "until we are exhausted, and then we shall attack again." Beyond these accomplishments, in December 1945 his expert defensive tactics helped stem the German push in the Ardennes.

Patton was a student of military history and fancied himself one of a long line of great warlords. On reaching Germany itself, he wrote in his journal: "Visited Trier, so did Caesar whose Gallic wars I am now reading. It is interesting to view in imagination the Roman legions marching down the same road."

After V-E Day, the day of German surrender, Patton, now military governor of Bavaria, found himself embroiled in new controversies. He came in for criticism for leniency toward former Nazis (he likened Nazis to members of American political parties; "Nazis Just Like the Republicans and Democrats" was how one headline summarized Patton's position) and for hostility toward the Soviets, who were still allies. "They are a scurvy race and simply savages," Patton said privately, "We could beat the hell out of them." Aghast, Eisenhower quickly relieved Patton of his duties and placed him in charge of the less important Fifteenth Army.

In December 1945 George Patton was killed in an automobile accident in Mannheim, Germany.

Perhaps the best known of all American generals was the flamboyant Patton. His heroics and foibles have been the subject of numerous books and films.

"Rommel has lost his nerve," Hitler complained. "He's become a pessimist. In these times only optimists can achieve anything." Rommel was indeed pessimistic and grew increasingly so as Hitler ignored von Rundstedt's suggestions for tactical withdrawals that would strengthen the *Wehrmacht*'s ability to resist the Allies. A frustrated von Rundstedt spoke openly of surrender ("Make peace, you fools"). When word of his defeatist comments reached Hitler, Hitler fired him.

The Death of Field Marshal Rommel

Rommel was marginally involved in an officers' plot to overthrow Hitler and end the war. As Germany continued to suffer reverse after reverse, many officers became convinced that Hitler must either be overthrown or killed in order to end the killing and destruction that was now being visited on Germany. Some even hoped that with the führer out of the way, Germany could negotiate a peace treaty with the western Allies and continue to fight on against the Soviet Union.

On July 20, 1944, Hitler attended a staff meeting at his eastern front headquarters, the *Wolfsschanze* ("Wolf's Lair"). There, Count Claus von Stauffenberg planted a powerful bomb just a few feet away from Hitler, which miraculously did not kill or even seriously harm him. In fact Hitler was able to keep an appointment later that afternoon with Italian dictator Benito Mussolini.

Despite Germany's reverses, Hitler still held an incredible emotional hold on the German people. With Hitler alive, the coup had no chance of success. The conspirators were rounded up one by one. To prolong their agony, Hitler ordered the main plotters hanged with piano wire. Before long Rommel was implicated in the plot. Because of Rommel's immense popularity Hitler hesitated to publicly charge him with involvement. Instead he gave the Desert Fox a choice: trial before the infamous People's Court and disgrace for himself and his family, or suicide. If Rommel committed suicide, he would be given a state funeral and his family would be left in peace. On October 14, 1944, Rommel, wearing his Afrika Korps jacket, took poison.

Battle of the Bulge

Throughout his career Hitler had been a gambler, both politically and militarily. Now, in a desperate attempt to put Germany on the offensive again, he bet *Wehrmacht* forces against the Allied line in northern France, which was particularly thin in the area between Monschau and the Moselle River. At this point Hitler would launch one last attack with the goal of capturing Liege and the port of Antwerp, disrupting the Allies' supply lines and inflicting a damaging blow on their morale.

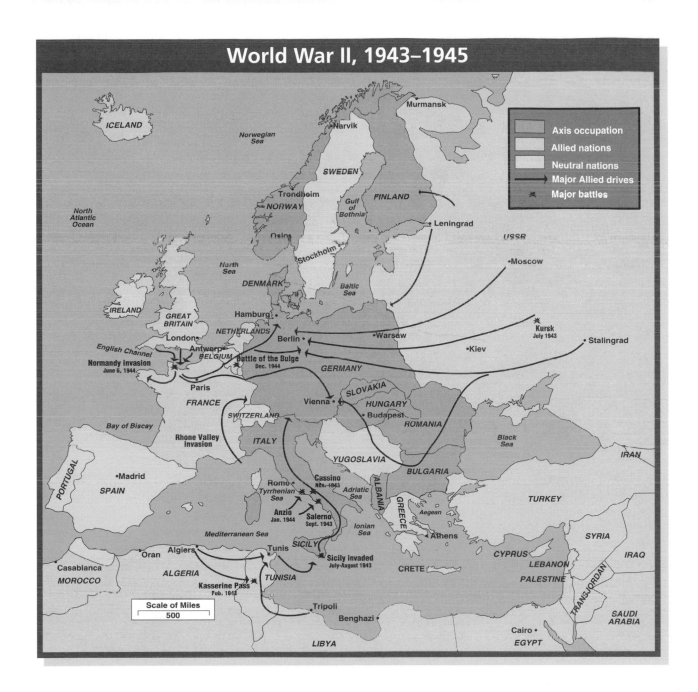

World War II, 1943–1945

Legend:
- Axis occupation
- Allied nations
- Neutral nations
- Major Allied drives
- Major battles

The Allies were aware of this risk but incorrectly thought no attack would occur. They theorized that the Germans were too weak for offensive action, and that in any case an attack through the Ardennes forest with winter approaching would be a difficult undertaking to pull off.

With a deep fog hampering Allied airpower, the Germans attacked on December 16, 1944, pushing the Allies back fifty miles (the bulge in their lines gave the engagement the title Battle of the Bulge) and virtually surrounding American forces at Bastogne in southeastern Belgium. The Germans, however, lacked the reserves

Though German troops kept up the fighting, obeying Hitler's command, an Allied victory was inevitable. Hitler's refusal to surrender meant a death sentence for thousands more of Germany's soldiers.

to capitalize on their advances and were slowly driven back. By January 25, 1945, the Allies had recaptured all the ground they had once lost.

The Germans had fought valiantly, but their losses from the Ardennes offensive were heavy: 250,000 men, 1,000 planes, and 600 tanks and assault guns. The allies lost 60,000 men. Never again would Germany be capable of another offensive.

Crossing the Rhine

The Germans still possessed one last great defense against the on-rushing British and American forces: the Rhine River. From Switzerland to the North Sea the mighty Rhine was a formidable natural barrier against Allied penetration of the German heartland.

Both Hitler and the Allies were well aware of the importance of the Rhine bridges. Hitler set out to destroy them all before the Allies could seize one; the Allies made capturing one their first priority. In early March 1945 Eisenhower launched Operation Lumberjack to drive toward the Rhine, and if possible cross it. On March 7 the Allies captured the one bridge spanning the Rhine that the Germans had not yet destroyed, at Remagen. Eisenhower ordered Bradley to put five divisions across the bridge as soon as he could. By March 23 the Allies had three

The Holocaust

The Nazis were not merely content to wage war on foreign armies. They also carried on a brutal war of extermination against their civilian "enemies."

Inmates of Nazi concentration camps ranged from socialists and communists to aristocratic noblemen and army officers, from homosexuals to Catholic priests, but their main targets were religious and ethnic minorities: Jews and Slavs.

Hitler, always a rabid anti-Semite, initiated his persecution of Germany's Jews as soon as he took power, but their mass slaughter did not begin until June 1941 when teams of *Einsatzgruppen* ("action squads") started shooting Jews in the conquered lands of eastern Europe.

By July 1942 the Nazis began the "final solution" to what they termed the "Jewish problem." The Nazis' goal was to exterminate every Jew within their reach. Before the Nazis were defeated, up to six million Jews died, many in horrible and sadistic concentration camps such as Auschwitz and Majdanek, where Jews were murdered in large gas chambers and their bodies burnt in massive crematoriums. Only at war's end did a shocked world fully learn of this immense holocaust.

Simon Wiesenthal, a former concentration camp inmate, spent decades tracking down Nazi war criminals. He has pointed out that the Holocaust did not include only six million persons. Actually, ten million died, including four million Gentiles, mostly Slavs, whom Hitler's "master race" (*herrenvolk*) of Germans regarded as "subhuman." Poland suffered the greatest loss in that regard, losing 22 percent of its entire prewar population (6,028,000 citizens) in the conflict. Half the dead were Polish Jews; the rest were Polish Christians.

Throughout Europe oppressed peoples rejoiced in the hope of liberation D day brought. In occupied Amsterdam, a fourteen-year-old Jewish girl named Anne Frank had by then spent almost two years hiding from the Nazis and in her diary expressed the elation millions felt.

The gruesome machinery of Hitler's systematic extermination plan.

"The best part of the invasion is that I have the feeling that friends are approaching," she wrote. "We have been oppressed by those terrible Germans for so long, they have had their knives so at our throats, that the thought of friends and delivery fills us with confidence! Now it doesn't concern the Jews any more; no, it concerns Holland and all occupied Europe. Perhaps . . . I may yet be able to go back to school in September or October."

The Allies came too late to save Anne Frank. In August 1944 the Germans discovered her family's hiding place and took them to the Belsen concentration camp, where Anne died in March 1945.

corps on the eastern side of the river in a beachhead twenty-five miles long and ten miles deep. On that date a general offensive across the Rhine was launched, driving deep into Germany itself.

The End of the Third Reich

While the British and Americans were streaming across France and into Germany, their Soviet allies were on the move, too. The Red Army had recaptured all the territory it had lost to Hitler, battled across Poland, Romania, Hungary, and Czechoslovakia and was advancing on Hitler's now-ruined capital of Berlin.

Although some say Hitler had known the war was lost since 1942, he had never publicly admitted defeat. In late April 1945 he was nearly surrounded by hostile armies. Germany's cities were destroyed. His *Wehrmacht* and *Luftwaffe* were virtually finished. Old men and young boys were now handed rifles and told to march off to face the advancing Allies.

Still Hitler prolonged the conflict as long as possible, causing the deaths of additional hundreds of thousands of persons. Then, trapped in his underground bunker, beneath the rubble of Berlin, he committed suicide on the night of April 30, 1945.

By May 1945 the western Allies had 4 million men at arms on the European continent: 2,585,000 Americans, 1,073,000 Commonwealth forces, 413,000 French, and 67,000 others. The Germans had little left to fight with. At 0241 on the morning of May 7 General Alfred Jodl signed the German surrender.

The killing in Europe begun on September 1, 1939, could now stop. The landings at D day had helped make that possible.

Glossary

Afrika Korps: German forces in North Africa under the command of General (later Field Marshal) Erwin Rommel.

Anschluss: the 1930s movement for Austrian unification with Germany that led to Austrian forced incorporation into Nazi Germany on March 12, 1938; the German word *anschluss* means "union" or "connection."

beachhead: the shore area captured by an attacking force in an amphibious invasion.

DUKW: a 2.5-ton amphibious truck introduced into combat by the United States at Kwajalein in the South Pacific.

Free French: those French citizens who continued to organize resistance to the Germans after their country was overrun in 1940.

glider: an engineless plane that is towed by a larger plane, released, and which then glides down to earth; especially useful when a silent landing is required.

Kriegsmarine: the German navy.

LCT (Landing Craft, Tank): a naval craft used to ferry Allied tanks, amphibious vehicles, combat vehicles, and equipment from ships to shore in an amphibious invasion; the first LCTs were commissioned in the South Pacific in December 1942.

LSA (Landing Ship, Assault): an assault ship that is designed for fairly long sea voyages and for rapid loading and unloading of troops in an amphibious operation.

Luftwaffe: the German air force.

Mulberries: the code name given by the Allies to two artificial harbors towed from England and used at Normandy until the port of Cherbourg was captured.

National Socialism: often called Nazism; the German ruling political philosophy from 1933 to 1945 as developed by Adolf Hitler; combined racism, expansionism, and anti-Semitism; the official name of the Nazi Party was the National Socialist German Workers Party (abbreviated as NSDAP in German).

OB West: the German High Command in western Europe; under the control of Field Marshal von Rundstedt at the time of the Normandy invasion.

OKW: *Oberkommando der Wehrmacht* (Armed Forces High Command); the German general staff.

panzer: the German word for armor; *Panzerwagon* is the actual German word for tank but this is most often shortened to panzer.

paratrooper: a soldier who parachutes into battle in an airborne operation.

SHAEF: Supreme Headquarters Allied Expeditionary Force; the office of Supreme Commander of the Allied invasion force, General Dwight D. Eisenhower.

SS: abbreviation for *Schutzstaffel* (German for "protective forces"), the elite corps of the Nazi Party; it eventually took on such tasks as guarding German death camps and of forming a segment of the German armed forces; the latter forces were known as the *Waffen* ("armed") *SS.*

Wehrmacht: the German armed forces, including the army, navy, and air force; the word is most often used, however, to describe the German army.

For Further Reading

Bruce Bliven Jr., *The Story of D-Day: June 6, 1944*. New York: Landmark Books, 1956. One of the earlier juvenile accounts of the invasion, but still an excellent reference. Highly recommended for adults as well.

Hodding Carter, *The Commandos of World War II*. New York: Random House, 1966. An overview of commandos during the conflict, with a look at the Normandy invasion.

Delos Lovelace, *"Ike" Eisenhower: Statesman and Soldier of Peace*. New York: Thomas Y. Crowell, 1961. Originally written during the war, this volume was updated to include Eisenhower's presidential career.

Albert Marrin, *Overlord: D-Day and the Invasion of Europe*. New York: Atheneum, 1982. A well-illustrated study of Normandy.

Alfred Steinberg, *Dwight David Eisenhower*. New York: G.P. Putnam's Sons, 1967. A serviceable look at Dwight Eisenhower's long career of public service.

Author's Note: I also recommend the following nontext sources regarding the Battle of Normandy and the Second World War.

Motion Pictures:

Fortitude (1994) Michael Caine, Gary Cole, and Catharine Predier. A look at D day from a perspective not usually examined—that of the French in Normandy. Made for television.

The Longest Day (1972) John Wayne, Henry Fonda, Robert Ryan, Red Buttons, Richard Burton, Richard Todd, Mel Ferrer, Alexander Knox, Curt Jurgens. Directors: Andrew Marton (U.S.), Bernhard Wicki (Germany), and Ken Annakin (UK). A star-studded but faithful account of Cornelius Ryan's classic book, which describes this enormous operation in vividly human terms.

Patton (1970) George C. Scott and Karl Malden. Directed by Franklin Schaffner. An excellent look at controversial general George S. Patton, which explains why Patton so consistently found himself in trouble with his superiors. Scott was magnificent in the title role. Both Scott and the film itself won Academy Awards.

CD-ROM:

Normandy: The Great Crusade, Discovery Communications, Inc., Bethesda, MD, 1994. An interesting and handsome learning tool developed by cable television's Discovery Channel. It lacks easy search capabilities and, considering the possibilities of the CD-ROM format, is weak on the amount of text available, but nonetheless provides impressive amounts of narration, archival film, and photographs.

Works Consulted

Douglas Botting, *The Second Front*. Alexandria, VA: Time-Life Books, 1978. A heavily illustrated volume on the Normandy invasion, with emphasis on the weapons of the operation. Part of a Time-Life series on World War II.

Omar N. Bradley and Clay Blair, *A General's Life*. New York: Simon and Schuster, 1983. Bradley's memoirs, which cover service in several wars. His dislike of General Patton is apparent after several decades.

Winston S. Churchill, *The Second World War: Closing the Ring*. Boston: Houghton Mifflin, 1951. Churchill provides an overview of World War II's final years.

Napier Crookenden, *Dropzone Normandy*. New York: Charles Scribner's Sons, 1976. An account of paratroop operations in Normandy, with emphasis on British units.

David Eisenhower, *Eisenhower at War 1943–1945*. New York: Random House, 1986. A well-researched study of Eisenhower during and after the Normandy invasion, by his grandson.

Max Hastings, *Overlord: D-Day, June 6, 1944*. New York: Simon and Schuster, 1984. A workmanlike study of the Allied operation and German countermoves.

Edwin P. Hoyt, *The Invasion Before Normandy: The Secret Battle of Slapton Sands*. New York: Stein and Day, 1985. The story of a little-known disaster that preceded the Normandy invasion.

John Keegan, *Six Armies in Normandy: From D-Day to the Liberation of Paris*. New York: Viking, 1982. A well-written description of operations in the Normandy peninsula with emphasis on the battles that raged after the beachhead was secured.

John Lukacs, *The Duel: 10 May–31 July 1940: The Eighty-Day Struggle Between Churchill and Hitler*. New York: Ticknor & Fields, 1990. A short volume on the months that saw Britain closest to defeat.

———, *The Last European War: September 1939–December 1941*. Garden City, NY: Anchor Press/Doubleday, 1976. A lengthy but worthwhile account of the beginning years of World War II by a masterful and eloquent historian.

John Man, *The D-Day Atlas: The Definitive Account of the Allied Invasion of Normandy*. New York: Facts On File, 1994. A well-organized small volume on D day. Filled with invaluable maps.

George S. Patton Jr., *War As I Knew It*. Boston: Houghton Mifflin, 1947. These memoirs, edited and published after Patton's death, have a patchwork, extremely hard-to-read aspect to them.

Werner Rings, *Life with the Enemy: Collaboration and Resistance in Hitler's Europe*. Garden City, NY: Doubleday, 1982. A fascinating and thought-provoking analysis of the choices made by those under Nazi occupation.

Friedrich Ruge, *Rommel in Normandy*. San Rafael, CA: Presidio Press, 1979. The story of Rommel's preparations for the invasion, told by his chief naval aide.

Cornelius Ryan, *The Longest Day*. New York: Simon and Schuster, 1959. The most famous book about the Normandy invasion, told with an emphasis on the individuals involved. Later made into a highly successful motion picture.

Walter Bedell Smith, *Eisenhower's Six Great Decisions*. New York: Longman's, Green, 1956. A brief volume on the most difficult choices made by Eisenhower as a military commander, written by one of his closest aides.

John Toland, *Adolf Hitler*. Garden City, NY: Doubleday, 1976. A classic biography of the German dictator.

Warren Tute, *D Day*. New York: Macmillan, 1974. A solid study of the invasion.

H.P. Willmott, *June 1944*. Poole, UK: Blandford Press, 1984. A book that looks at not only the Normandy invasion but what was transpiring on the war's other fronts as well.

Robert Wistrich, *Who's Who in Nazi Germany*. New York: Bonanza Books, 1984. Interesting background on many of those involved on the German side.

Index

Picture Credits

Cover photo by The Bettmann Archive

AP/Wide World Photos, 43 (top), 51 (top), 73 (top), 79, 81

The Bettman Archive, 10, 46, 53, 97

Library of Congress, 18, 21, 38 (both), 87, 91

National Archives, 11 (both), 12, 13, 15, 16 (top), 19, 20, 23 (both), 24, 25, 31, 33 (both), 34, 36, 42, 44, 45, 49 (top), 51 (bottom), 54 (both), 56, 62, 70, 74, 75, 78, 82, 84 (both), 85, 89, 94 (bottom), 95, 100, 101, 102

Simon Wiesenthal Center, 16 (bottom)

UPI/Bettmann, 27, 28, 41, 43 (bottom), 49 (bottom), 50, 61, 64, 68, 69, 73 (bottom), 90, 92, 93, 94 (top and middle)

About the Author

David Pietrusza has written for numerous publications, including *Modern Age, The Journal of Social & Political Studies, Academic Reviewer,* and *The New Oxford Review.* For two years he produced the nationally syndicated radio program *National Perspectives.* His other Lucent titles include *The End of the Cold War, The Battle of Waterloo,* and the forthcoming *The Mysterious Death of John F. Kennedy.*

Mr. Pietrusza has also written extensively on the subject of baseball. He is the president of the Society for American Baseball Research (SABR) and managing editor of *Total Baseball.* His three books on baseball are *Minor Miracles, Major Leagues,* and *Baseball's Canadian-American League,* and he is working on a history of night baseball. In 1994 he served as a consultant for the PBS Learning Link system and produced the documentary *Local Heroes* for PBS affiliate WMHT.

He lives with his wife, Patricia, in Scotia, New York.